Rescue,

Rebuild,

Restore

Compassion That Works

Suzanne Burns

Rescue, Rebuild, Restore: Compassion That Works

Copyright © 2025. BeCharityWise. All rights reserved. No part of this book may be reproduced by any mechanical, photographic, or electronic process, or in the form of a phonographic recording; nor may it be stored in a retrieval system, transmitted, or otherwise be copied for public or private use—other than for "fair use" as brief quotations embodied in articles and reviews—without prior written permission of the publisher.
ISBN: 979-8-9852088-8-7
Design and cover art by Ashley Neer.

This publication is designed to provide accurate and authoritative information regarding the subject matter covered. It is sold with the understanding that the publisher is not engaged in rendering legal, accounting, or other professional services. If you require legal advice or other expert assistance, you should seek the services of a competent professional.

Disclaimer: The author makes no guarantees to the results you'll achieve by reading this book. All business requires risk and hard work. The results and client case studies presented in this book represent results achieved working directly with the author. Your results may vary when undertaking any new business venture or marketing strategy.

Dedication

This book is dedicated, first, to my family. You have all sacrificed so much as I have chased after the Lord in founding a maternity home. Thank you!

To the staff, board, and volunteers of Foundation House Ministries, without whom none of this would be possible. I am so very proud of you!

Rescue Rebuild Restore

Quote

No Good Deed Goes Unpunished.
~Oscar Wilde~

Table of Contents

Introduction

Part 1: The Times, They Are A-Changing

    Chapter 1: A New Reality

    Chapter 2: Are You My People?

    Chapter 3: Givers and Receivers

    Chapter 4: Counting the Cost, Love Never Fails

    Chapter 5: The Catch

Part 2: Rescue, Rebuild, Restore

    Chapter 6: Wisdom to Understand

    Chapter 7: Rescue

    Chapter 8: Rebuild

    Chapter 9: Restore

Part 3: How Now Shall We Live?

    Chapter 11: Are You Safe?

    Chapter 12: What Is Our Actual Goal?

    Chapter 13: Living the Framework—Implementing Rescue, Rebuild, Restore for Lasting Impact

    Next Steps

    About the Author

Introduction

Dear reader,

As followers of Christ, we are called to love the least of these with compassion, wisdom, and unwavering faith—meeting their deepest needs amidst poverty, trauma, addiction, and mental health challenges. *Rescue, Rebuild, Restore: Compassion That Works* is your companion on this sacred journey, rooted in the RRR framework, which emphasizes individualized care, trust in the Holy Spirit, and practical action.

This book emerges from my experiences at Foundation House, where we've learned to navigate the complexities of serving mothers and families in crisis, guided by God's love. Through the Rescue, Rebuild, Restore Framework, we'll explore how to rescue those drowning in despair, rebuild their lives with self-efficacy and trust, and restore hope for lasting transformation. Each chapter builds on biblical wisdom—such as Matthew 25:40, "Whatever you did for one of the least of these brothers and sisters of mine, you did for me"—and practical insights, addressing the unique stories shaped by poverty mindsets, trauma responses, addiction struggles, and mental health needs.

Rescue Rebuild Restore

You have your own specific assignment from the Lord, a group of people you are called to serve. It may be your own neighborhood, or a housing complex full of wild, funny, dirty, hungry, resilient children. Or maybe you feel drawn to the homeless you see walking up and down your streets, sometimes arguing with the wind, sometimes carting their worldly possessions in a buggy they stole from Walmart.

Maybe you, like me, long to see young families find hope and healing in Jesus rather than drugs. You may pray for opportunities to help young men understand what it means to be husbands and fathers, battling against the rampant, destructive fatherlessness that permeates our culture.

Chances are, if you've been working with people in need for very long, you've seen a variety of harmful behaviors, attitudes, and responses toward your efforts, which have left you frustrated, disappointed, and confused.

For some, these hurtful attitudes toward your best efforts have caused you to pull back, either from specific people or from helping in general.

I want to help you understand why people think and behave the way that they do. With this knowledge, you'll be better equipped to serve them in wisdom—meeting their needs in love without feeling manipulated, abused, or taken advantage of.

When you're working with people in chronic need, there are a few underlying characteristics which transcend age, race, ethnicity, or low socio-economic status. Once you understand the principles, you will be empowered to battle the enemy of our souls, on behalf of those you've been called to serve.

Whether you're a church member, volunteer, or ministry leader, you'll find tools to serve wisely, avoiding pitfalls like judgment, control, or burnout. We'll uncover the cost of unconditional love (Chapter 4), the myths that trap us (Chapter 5), and the emotional cycles of change (Chapter 8), equipping you to partner with God and each receiver for eternal impact.

As you read, reflect on the people you serve or hope to serve—looking for similarities, nuances, and areas for growth. Hold everything loosely, trusting the Lord to guide you, as no two journeys are alike. This book isn't a manual for perfection but a call to love as Jesus does, with patience, grace, and rugged individualism. Let us pray for the courage to anchor in His love, stabilize in His wisdom, and reach out with hope, transforming lives one heart at a time.

My heart's desire, as you read these pages, is for you to fall passionately in love with a group of people, so passionately that you are willing to lay down your self-interests, your false beliefs, and your ego in order to serve them as Jesus did. I want you to join me in rescuing, rebuilding, and restoring even more people—moms, dads, kids, families. Souls who need your help to discover the fullness of the promises of God, on this earth as well as in the Life to come.

And also, I want you to feel confident that you are equipped for what that servant ministry will actually require of you.

Within the pages of this book, you will learn:
- Why they act the way they do.
- Why they are worth your willing self-sacrifice.
- How badly the odds have been stacked against them.
- How deeply the Lord loves them and how terribly they've been deceived by the enemy of our souls.
- What you can do to help—in large and small ways.

One of those ways that you can help the people you are called to serve is through hiring my team and me to train and equip you in the Rescue, Rebuild, Restore Framework, and I will tell you much more about that throughout this book.

Within these pages, I'll be sharing stories—my own, my staff, my clients, my friends.

All of these stories I have permission to use; however, there are a few where I've changed names and a few specific details, for her privacy. When that happens, you'll see an * by her name.

And a note: Even if you live near our maternity home in southeastern Tennessee and you meet one of the moms mentioned in this book, I ask that you not bring up these stories directly to her.

Knowing her story and hearing it spoken back to her are two very different things. I'm sure you wouldn't intend to speak in a way that would hurt her, yet nevertheless, the enemy is always seeking ways to kill, steal, and destroy. You never know what he is whispering in her ear at that moment. Pray for her and encourage her, but please don't dredge up her past unless she brings it up herself.

You can learn more about my ministry at https://foundationhouseministries.org

And if you'd like to go ahead and schedule a call with me to discuss what training for your team could look like, please do! I'd love to talk with you.

Here's a link to schedule a call with me:
https://calendly.com/suzanne-bcw/call-from-book
I'm looking forward to hearing from you!
With love,
Suzanne Burns

Part 1: The Times, They Are A-Changing

Pure and undefiled religion is this: to look after the widows and orphans in their distress.
James 1:27

Chapter 1: A New Reality

When I first started the maternity home I still lead today, I thought the women I would serve would be a lot like myself. I had my own story of single-mom struggles, then dating-mom struggles, and then I discovered how to navigate the unique challenges of life in a blended family. I had some college, some job skills, and a mostly-healthy family support system who loved me and my little ones. And still, those were very difficult years.

I knew I had the experience and the wisdom to help other girls who found themselves in the same situation I had once been in. I trusted that I could meet their needs. By the time we launched our residential ministry in 2014, I thought we were ready for our first client. We had a bed for her. We had a curriculum. We had a plan. I love plans...

But it turned out that I had no idea what the needs of these girls *really* were. I didn't understand why our very first client didn't see the value in the job-training and GED prep classes we sought out for her. Shay* didn't care about any of it. She was homeless with her two-week-old son when she arrived—the very first client Foundation House Ministries ever housed (though we had already worked with a handful of others, staying in the homeless shelter or motel rooms). And yet, her attitude, from the beginning, frustrated me.

Not only was she not grateful for anything we did, she made it clear, in not so subtle ways, that what we were doing wasn't good enough. We provided all her transportation, anywhere she needed to go. We housed and fed her and helped her get the things she needed for her son. We watched little D* while she worked, until we found childcare. We provided for 100% of her needs so she could save her money and prepare to build a stable life. That was the goal.

However, she also didn't appreciate me asking to see her bank statements. She didn't understand why I should see something so private. So personal.

When she left our home a few months later, it took two SUV-loads to haul her and her infant son's things from our home. Turns out, the reason she wouldn't share her bank info was that she hadn't saved a single penny. She'd spent everything she'd earned and had nothing but *stuff* to show for it.

From our home, she moved back into low-income government housing with her mom, the exact place where she had been kicked out just a few months prior, the reason she had entered our fledgling program to begin with.

She hadn't saved a penny.
- She was back in the same toxic home environment.
- Her life had not changed one bit.

She was back in the exact same situation as before she arrived.

Not merely a similar one.

Exactly. The. Same. Place.

Our little fledgling ministry had benefited her exactly zero.

I felt like a failure. I had tried so hard to teach her what I knew she needed to know. And I watched, firsthand, as it all went in one ear and right out the other.

I had not benefited her in any real, tangible way. Devastated, I nearly closed the ministry.

But the Lord challenged me to keep going, to learn and grow. I persevered and soon He brought me a book called *Toxic Charity*, which taught me about the toxic relationship that can develop between people in poverty and those trying to help them.

I learned that we helpers can develop a savior mentality, an assumption that we are right, that we know everything. We can become so caught up in *doing for* those who are in need that those we are "helping" actually get trained to just sit back and let us do all the work. They don't learn how to do things for themselves because we're too busy doing it for them. And then, we helpers get frustrated and disheartened when nothing seems to change in the lives of the people we serve. Completely unaware that <u>we caused that exact response by our own actions.</u>

That prompted some *deep* soul searching.

Then I read *When Helping Hurts*, another fantastic book by my friends at The Chalmers Center. (Turns out, they live less than an hour from me and we've become good friends over the years!)

This is where I began to open my eyes to the unhealthy relationships I had built with my clients. I had seen this pattern in the actions of other clients I worked with before Shay arrived, such as a mother and pregnant daughter duo I met. They were sweet, precious people, but their mindset was that it was easier to locate $40 a night to stay in a hotel room than it was to get jobs and earn a stable income.

Through these and other interactions, I fell into the trap of attributing the problems I observed to the <u>people I was helping</u>, certainly not the way in which I had built my ministry…

Turns out, *it was me*. Not them.

Well, it was also definitely them; let's not swing the pendulum too far in the opposite direction. I was not responsible for the situations they found themselves in or their responses. What I *was* responsible for was inadvertently developing a system of support which <u>played into</u> their trained behaviors, which they had learned by working with other organizations. I just set myself up for a repeat of everything they'd experienced in the past. And so I received back a repetition of behaviors and attitudes that were both unhelpful and also made perfect sense, from the perspective of my client's survival.

Reading these two books, so early in my ministry, radically transformed the kind of relationships we would build with our clients.

We learned how to do it differently.

It has not been easy, these last 10 years, building a new paradigm. A new way to serve our homeless, pregnant or parenting, mamas. A new way to build life transformation and personal accountability into their daily lives. Many of our early clients moved into our home and then moved right back out, within days or weeks.

It was a lot of trial and error, at first. And then, in 2017, the Lord brought me another book, this time on the lasting physical effects of trauma.

Rescue Rebuild Restore

Within the pages of *The Body Keeps the Score*, by Bessel van der Kolk, I finally discovered the crucial linchpin issue, which **fed** the other major pieces: poverty mindset, addiction, abuse, and mental health struggles.

I finally understood what was really happening inside the bodies and minds of each of our clients. The traumatic situations they had endured had left behind the ravages of toxic stress, which continues to affect body, mind, and spirit, until healing takes place.

And it was from this new knowledge that the Lord birthed the solutions we developed, again, very much through trial and error (ours, not His) until we began to understand how to help these women at their deepest core, attacking the root structure of all that had harmed them throughout their young lives.

I'll share all of that with you later in the book. In Part 2, to be exact.

And the most beautiful part is that this applies not just to the mamas that my team and I serve, but to everyone you meet with a history of trauma, addiction, and abuse. Whether your mission is moms in crisis or low income families or homeless vets, or even just friends or family members, you'll find understanding, knowledge, and experience within these pages.

And then, in Part 3, I'll give you some tips, tools, and strategies that you can immediately begin using as you love the "least of these" in your community. But first, I want to help you understand a bit more about the struggles of the people you serve—why they do the things they do, how they get into these terrible situations in the first place.

Over the past decade, we've housed over 150 moms and their children and worked with more than 900 other families, mostly single moms but also a handful of married couples and single dads as well, through our nonresidential support services.

When I say we've learned from every client, every situation, we absolutely have. We've seen a lot of success. In fact, we boast a 97% success rate of those who <u>graduate</u> our program maintaining their level of personal stability for at least a year after they graduate. And 85% are still maintaining their stability five years later.

But that's not to say that every client who arrives will also graduate. We've also seen plenty of women return to their old lifestyles of drugs, domestic violence, loss of custody of their children, and even loss of life to overdose or violence.

It's a challenging place to work, but it's a beautiful place, too. Beautiful chaos. But so very worth it.

This is absolutely not a "sunshine and roses" type of book, but rather one that (I hope) encourages you to run with me in this race to rescue a generation, to love them into the arms of Jesus, the only place where they'll find true freedom, true fulfillment, true joy. True love.

Before we dive too deeply into everything I want to share with you, I first want to introduce you to a couple of my dear friends. Graduates of our ministry, these three ladies are now also on permanent staff with us. They are remarkable. They've persevered. It has definitely not been easy, but they are three of the biggest successes we've seen and I love them dearly.

Ashley: Ashley arrived eight months pregnant, fresh out of six months in jail. I'll never forget the huge purple dreads in this little white girl's hair. She was bitter over being wrongfully accused, yet she knew the slippery slope she'd been walking along. Now she's happily married and serves as our Assistant Director of Client Services.

Morgan: I'll never forget the day she threw a toddler-style temper tantrum in the thrift shop, at the shoulda-known-better age of 27. She needed to be brought to her lowest point, forced to fight or give up her daughter forever. Morgan found a core of strength and commitment that she couldn't have discovered another way. Today, Morgan works in our case management department, ministering to other girls daily.

Brooke: Bless her heart, she's lived a lifetime of addiction, mental health challenges, cognitive delays, and abandonment. Today, she is living her best life as a shift supervisor in our job-training program, training new girls in our systems and celebrating four years of sobriety. She'll probably still be living with us when Jesus comes back.

Now that you've seen a bit about how our Rescue, Rebuild, Restore approach can radically transform the lives of the people you serve, I want to shift gears in Chapter 2.

Let's talk next about what *you* will need in order to pull off these kinds of transformational stories.

Chapter 2: Are You My People?

"the hands and feet of Jesus"

My assumption, because you picked up this book, is that you are already a compassionate Christian. Someone who desires to love "the least of these."

But are you loving *wisely*?

When you see someone holding a cardboard sign along the off-ramp, do you give them cash? Food? Directions to the nearest shelter?

Have you paid for a motel room for someone in crisis, so they would have a safe place to sleep, only to discover that they expected you to *keep* paying for their room? Or, worse, that they were prostituting out of it?

Yeah, this book is gonna be *that* real.

Has your church taken up a sacrificial love offering to pay for a young single mom's car repairs, only for her to ask you to pay for something *else* a few weeks later?

When does it end? Why isn't she grateful? How do you help without being manipulated or taken advantage of?

Short answer: you don't.

Spoiler: You're going to have to accept some level of attempted manipulation, if you want to work with people in long-term crisis mode. It comes with the territory.

People in chronic crisis, which is virtually everyone you see begging along the interstate or calling your church office, are also in chronic survival mode. And it is that chronic survival mode which creates those frustrating behaviors and attitudes which so often disappoint kindhearted people, causing them to feel misused, which then leads them to reject future opportunities to love and serve the least of these. Thus perpetuating the cycle of over-helping, hurt, and eventual abandonment in those who are yet to come.

Too often I see churches over-give and then regret it. No amount of compassion or money seems to be enough for some clients. Churches are routinely called or visited by people looking for a handout. Help with this month's rent. Groceries. Shoes. One of my former pastors, who has since passed away, took off his shoes early one Sunday morning to give to a homeless person who had stopped by the little country church we attended. He then proceeded to preach that morning's message in his socks.

That is overabundant compassion.

He felt that was what the Lord asked of him that morning. And so it brought him pleasure to be obedient in the sacrifice. But he never saw that man again. That may have been all he was assigned to do for that particular person, but also there may have been other things that he could've done, if he had begun to build a relationship.

I remember a client of ours years ago. Alli* had been attending another little country church while she was homeless and pregnant. When she came into our residential program, she already had a car, in poor condition, but we allowed her to continue to drive to that specific church. She had already established that relationship and we didn't want to damage it by setting arbitrary obstacles in her way.

Not too long after she moved into our little house, we got a call from the church. They had taken up a love offering to help Alli* pay for repairs to her car. They had sacrificially raised over $2000, a vast amount for this tiny congregation. We cautioned them that this was not the best use of their money, that she didn't need the repairs, not yet, and that she wouldn't be grateful. A couple weeks later, that same pastor called us again, this time angry because Alli had asked the church to buy her new tires, also.

We knew exactly how that situation was going to turn out. But the little church hadn't wanted to hear what we had to say. And then, when they felt mistreated, taken advantage of, they wanted to cut ties with our girl, Alli. She couldn't understand why the church would suddenly refuse to help her, why they didn't love her anymore. She was heartbroken and devastated. And she refused to darken another church's doors for many years.

That's the fatal problem in all of this. The clients are only acting on what they've been trained, by the Church, to expect. That church changed its rules of engagement and the client didn't understand. And yet, it's all deeply tied to each person's ultimate acceptance or rejection of Jesus.

It is such a frustrating situation. I'm going to explain more about this unhealthy dynamic in Chapter 3 and then, in Chapter 6, you'll understand WHY.

A quick note right here: when you see "church" with a small c, I'm referring to a specific congregation. When you see

"Church," I'm referring to the whole Body of Christ, transcending congregations and denominations. We're all in this together, part of the problem and also potential to be part of the solution.

Here's one more example for you. A number of years ago, at the little church I attended where the pastor preached in his sock-feet, there was a couple who regularly struggled financially. I knew them well. She worked for me and our husbands also worked together. I share their story in one of my early books, *The Accidental Social Worker*. I'll call them Carl and Tammy.

One day, they approached one of the deacons and asked if the church could help them pay their rent. They were short nearly all of it, and it was due in four days. This couple had been attending regularly for over a year and so the church elders agreed to help them. They were grateful as the church secretary made out a check to their landlord for the full amount.

And then, the following Sunday… Carl came bounding into the sanctuary, excited to show off the first phase of his new full-back tattoo.

Needless to say, several people in the church were furious. Carl and Tammy couldn't understand why their friends weren't more excited about Carl's new ink. It *did* look cool.

Now, in Carl and Tammy's defense, they had been pre-paying for this artwork for several months prior to this first round of tattoo work, so they had not lied to the church when they said they didn't have the money for rent. But yet, they seemed incapable of connecting the dots that other members of the congregation did… if they had disposable income to pay for a huge, multi-phase tattoo, then they had the money to pay their own rent. The tattoo was not a necessity. Rent definitely was.

But that's not how Carl and Tammy saw it.

These stories are just a few quick snapshots to help you see where we are heading within the coming chapters of this book.

By the time you finish, if you do, (I hope you do), then you'll understand exactly why Carl and Tammy, and also Alli, made decisions that seemed so inappropriate to the churches who sought to help them.

Poverty mindset is one of the first things we'll discuss when we get to Chapter 6. It's going to shed so much clarity on your most frustrating experiences.

But first, I want to be sure you understand the dynamics underlying these relationships, understand your role, your church's role, and also the role of the person you're seeking to serve.

In Chapter 3, I'd like to talk about some of the challenges you're likely already facing, even if you're not yet aware of them.

Self-Assessment: Understanding Your Approach to Need

Use this assessment to reflect on your understanding of receivers' needs. Rate each statement on a scale of 1-5 (1 = Strongly Disagree, 5 = Strongly Agree). Total your score to evaluate your approach and identify areas for growth.

- I recognize that poverty includes mindsets and systemic barriers, not just material lack, and I seek to address both.
- I understand how trauma, addiction, and mental health shape receivers' behaviors, avoiding judgment or quick fixes.
- I trust God to guide me in understanding receivers' unique stories, rather than assuming I know their needs.

- I am willing to partner with professionals or community resources to address complex needs like addiction or mental health.
- I avoid sustaining receivers with temporary aid, aiming instead to rescue, rebuild, and restore with long-term impact.
- I pray for discernment to see beyond surface struggles, listening to receivers' experiences with compassion.
- I hold expectations loosely, ready to tailor my ministry to each person's poverty, trauma, addiction, or mental health journey.
- I believe God can use my understanding to transform lives, even amidst challenges or setbacks.

Scoring:
- 8-16: You may need to deepen your understanding, seeking God's guidance to serve with greater insight.
- 17-32: You're on a good path, but there's room to refine your approach, focusing on empathy and partnership.
- 33-40: Your understanding is strong and faith-filled, but continue seeking His wisdom to sustain your ministry.

Chapter 3: Givers and Receivers

By now, as you've read the stories I shared in the last chapter, you're probably nodding your head in agreement. You've *been* one of those sweet churchgoers, giving sacrificially, only to be asked for yet more almost immediately.

Most of the kindhearted <u>givers</u> I've spoken with over the years have been burned. Manipulated. And then they're cursed at, mistreated when they inevitably *stop* giving, stop allowing themselves to be taken advantage of.

But, to be fair, the way the <u>receivers</u> describe how these situations play out often paints a vastly different picture. And it's in this contrast that we see the first real issue—lack of understanding the other person's perspective.

It was also through The Chalmers Center that I learned to think of people in categories of givers and receivers. This language can help us clarify who we are talking about, as well as typical responses from the two groups. In other words, this is language I use here within the pages of this book, or when I'm teaching a church or ministry my Rescue, Rebuild, Restore (RRR) Framework, but I would <u>*not*</u> use this language with an actual client. Instead, we approach each person with the love and respect Christ modeled, seeing them as individuals created in God's image.

Let me take just a moment to clarify exactly who and what I'm referring to, within this book.

Givers: Typically, these are individuals, churches, or ministries offering help or solutions to address the needs of receivers—whether through food, money, or other support.

Receivers: These are individuals or families seeking assistance, often expecting help due to past experiences, recommendations, or the giver's established systems of care.

So a Giver can be a single person or a group of people, even a dedicated ministry designed to serve the poor. And a Receiver approaches for help, with an expectation that their request will be met. Sometimes because they've received help from this Giver before, someone else recommended the Receiver contact this Giver for help, or the Giver has developed an organized system to serve more Receivers, more effectively.

This distinction helps us navigate the complexities of ministry, but it's only the beginning. We must move beyond labels to truly understand the hearts, struggles, and perspectives of both groups, guided by the Holy Spirit's wisdom.

Before we dive deeper, let's discuss three key assumptions about you, the reader, servant, giver:

Assumption #1: This is not your first rodeo.

For the sake of this book's focus, we're going to assume that you are operating as all three. You're an individual with thoughts, feelings and opinions, and a personal heart for giving. You serve through your church and you've been doing it long enough that you (and perhaps a team of like-minded people) have developed a system for community outreach and benevolence, even if it's not formally established as a separate and distinct ministry, beyond your church walls. People in need come to you often, looking for and expecting your assistance.

Assumption #2: You've been burned before.

If you've been serving other people for any length of time, you've experienced a situation (and probably more than one!) where you ended up feeling used, abused, mistreated or like you had "failed" that person or situation. Hurting people do tend to hurt people. And you've been hurt before.

Assumption #3: You're still healing but willing to keep serving.

This is the most crucial assumption. In order for you to benefit from this book, you have to be willing to serve again, in spite of the hurt you've experienced before. My goal is to help you understand why you were hurt, why the receivers behaved as they did, and how you can prevent, or at least protect yourself, from it happening in the future.

If my assumptions about you are correct, then let's dive in!

Let's start with the innermost thoughts of the givers, the category of most of you reading this book.

Hurdle #1 - Empathy, Sympathy, and Disappointment

I've already mentioned that the giver, in any help-gone-wrong situation, likely feels abused, mistreated, taken advantage of. We sometimes hear phrases like "got conned" or "snowed," often with a sense of righteous indignation. Givers often feel offended on behalf of their church, or Jesus, not just themselves, when things go wrong with a receiver.

Our compassion often stems from one of two places:

1. <u>Empathy</u>: Rooted in personal experience, where we've faced great lack and understand the struggle of needing help. Yet, this can lead us to expect others to overcome quickly, as we did, holding them to high standards that may feel unattainable. For example, a giver might think, "I survived homelessness and instability. They can, too," which can sound harsh or judgmental to a receiver, reinforcing their sense of hopelessness or inferiority.

2. <u>Sympathy</u>: Rooted in pity for someone's suffering, often because we haven't faced similar struggles. Sympathetic givers may give more—money, resources, time—longer than empathetic ones, but this can stem from "bypasser's guilt" or shame for their own comfort, which can harm both parties.

Many givers can recall times in their lives where they were the ones in need of someone else's generosity. Their compassion is rooted in empathy, understanding rooted in experience of how it feels to stand in the other person's shoes. Other givers may *not* have experienced similar situations. *Their* compassion is rooted in sympathy, or pity, for the other person.

It may seem counterintuitive, but, as a general rule, those givers who are operating from <u>sympathy</u> are oftentimes more willing to continue giving sacrificially for a longer period than those who are operating from a place of <u>empathy</u>, from an understanding rooted in experience. I think it is *because* the second group has experiential knowledge that they frequently appear to walk in less grace and mercy than those who've never walked in these types of difficulties.

Those empathetic ones have experienced great lack and learned how to survive, even thrive. Because they know it's possible, they can too often hold other people to higher expectations of how quickly someone should be able to overcome their current circumstances.

One of my former Board members said it like this, "I survived homelessness and abandonment while caring for young kids. It was hard but I survived. She can, too."

Yep. That is a true and accurate statement and yet, when spoken from a place of anger and disappointment, it becomes yet another reminder to the receiver that something in them must be flawed or broken.

A receiver hears this and thinks, "Others can overcome but I haven't been able to. I must be as worthless as everyone has told me, all my life." Thus reinforcing their sense of hopelessness and inferiority.

Even among other receivers, we see this lack of empathy play out. We consistently see a lack of empathy in our clients' attitudes toward new clients coming into the program. There's an underlying fear that, if we give something to this new client, it will diminish what we have available for the client who has been with us longer. Nothing could be further from the truth, but she doesn't yet know the endless love of Jesus. She only knows a life of lack, of survival of the strongest.

What about those who are *sympathetic*? Surely this is more helpful, since they tend to give more and longer than those who are empathetic, right? Well, they do tend to give more—money and things—for a longer period of time before they give up. But what is happening underneath the surface looks more like pity than anything useful. There's often a feeling of "survivor's guilt," or maybe more accurately "bypasser's guilt," shame for their relative comfort and success, because they've never had to endure these types of suffering. Which is equally harmful but harder to combat, as few sympathetic givers are willing to let someone free them of the weight of that guilt.

I've found that we Christians tend to carry some degree of guilt. Maybe we think that protects us against pride and arrogance. But in reality, all it does is focus our attention on ourselves, reinforcing our self-absorption...

That's not helpful.

Before we move to the next obstacle facing you, as you serve the least of these, I want to address how the receiver generally perceives these situations.

Receivers who have been in chronic need have already had many interactions with kindhearted people over the years. And yet they're still in the same position. They've survived but they haven't learned how to thrive, how to build a new life for themselves.

Receivers tend to have expectations about how the church should help them and also how the church people are going to judge them. As a general rule, they're right—at least about how church members tend to view the dirty, hungry, unhappy among them.

Self-Assessment: Evaluating Your Heart for Giving

Use this assessment to reflect on your approach to giving. Rate each statement on a scale of 1-5 (1 = Strongly Disagree, 5 = Strongly Agree). Total your score at the end to gauge your current mindset and identify areas for growth.

- I often feel empathy for receivers because I've experienced similar struggles in my own life.

- I tend to give out of sympathy, feeling pity for those in need, even if I haven't faced their challenges.
- I sometimes expect receivers to overcome their circumstances as quickly as I or others have, which may lead to frustration.
- I feel disappointed or hurt when receivers don't respond as I hoped, and it affects my willingness to continue giving.
- I regularly pray for God's wisdom to guide my compassion, whether it's rooted in empathy or sympathy.
- I recognize when my giving might stem from guilt or a desire to be a "savior," and I seek to align it with Christ's love.
- I actively listen to receivers' stories to understand their perspective, rather than assuming I know their needs.
- I trust God to heal both me and the receiver, even when our interactions feel challenging or painful.

Scoring:
- 8-16: You may need to deepen your understanding of empathy and sympathy, seeking God's guidance to serve with greater grace.
- 17-32: You're on a good path, but there's room to refine your approach, balancing empathy and sympathy with prayerful discernment.
- 33-40: Your heart for giving is strong and aligned with God's love, but continue seeking His wisdom to sustain your compassion.

Hurdle #2 - Cross-Purposes

Each person is coming into this connection with an underlying motive. And these motives often work at cross-purposes. Givers may be working to assuage their "Christian guilt" or may enjoy feeling like a hero, a "savior mentality" which can rapidly become harmful.

A receiver has many needs, and oftentimes, what they ask for (or what you're prepared to give) does not actually make a true dent into their real need. So, weeds of bitterness, resentment, greed, and envy can find fertile ground in which to grow. And also, this lifestyle of perpetual lack, this never-enough reality can also deepen roots of hopelessness and inferiority.

So a "savior" wannabe and a hopeless, helpless, needy person can birth a damaging, codependent relationship which reinforces the worst aspects of each of them. Until one or the other takes it too far, crosses a hidden boundary, and it all blows up, leaving everyone devastated, confused, and oftentimes, very angry.

How do you combat this? Carefully.

There's this underlying balancing act, this careful balancing of the position of power, authority on the part of the giver, doling out a prescribed solution to the receiver's problem.

You've got to be careful not to over-give and reinforce the receiver's sense of personal helplessness. And yet, also, you have to reconcile yourself to the fact that whatever you do is (most likely) not going to move the receiver completely out of their present circumstances. Check your expectations. Your box of food or your $20 bill, even your $100 bill, will not demonstrably move them out of their chronic crisis lifestyle.

You, the giver, must be able to see the bigger picture so that you can navigate this delicate balancing act in wisdom and grace.

We'll discuss this in far more detail in Part 2, but for now I want to touch on one more common obstacle to implementing

Self-Assessment: Aligning Motives and Expectations

Use this assessment to reflect on your motives and expectations as a giver. Rate each statement on a scale of 1-5 (1 = Strongly Disagree, 5 = Strongly Agree). Total your score to evaluate your alignment with God's purpose.

- I sometimes give to ease my own guilt or feel like a hero, rather than out of love for Christ and the receiver.
- I recognize when my expectations for receivers (e.g., quick change) don't match their real needs or capacities.
- I feel frustrated or hurt when receivers don't use my help as I intended, and it affects our relationship.
- I regularly pray for God to reveal the true needs of receivers, beyond what they ask for or what I assume.
- I check my "savior mentality" by seeking to partner with receivers, not control their outcomes.
- I trust God to work through small acts of giving (like food or money) to build trust, even if change is gradual.
- I'm willing to set healthy boundaries with receivers to prevent codependency, guided by prayer and wisdom.

Scoring:

- 7-14: You may need to examine your motives and expectations, seeking God's guidance to serve with humility and patience.
- 15-28: You're making progress, but there's room to refine your approach, focusing on partnership over control.

- 29-35: Your motives and expectations are well-aligned with God's heart, but continue seeking His wisdom to sustain your ministry.

Hurdle #3 - Entrenched Beliefs and Expectations

Our beliefs about receivers—and theirs about us—can shape our interactions profoundly. As givers, we must ask: What do we truly think about those coming to us in need? Do we see them as poor, helpless, lost souls, or as people capable of change, even if they've made poor decisions? Our mindset directly affects how we treat them.

A. <u>The Givers</u>

What do you *really* think about the people coming to you, in need? Do you see a poor, helpless, lost soul? Do you see someone who made poor decisions and is now living with the consequences of those decisions? Do you see somebody who could and should be making better decisions? What do you think? Are they helpless to change or are they capable of change but choosing not to? Yet, as Scripture reminds us, "If there is still breath, there is still hope" (Job 14:7, paraphrased).

This pulls us into a conversation about growth versus fixed mindsets. A growth mindset is one in which a person realizes they are able to learn and change, to grow and progress forward. A growth mindset, rooted in faith, sees potential for transformation, offering opportunities for learning, change, and progress, even amidst poverty, trauma, addiction, or mental health challenges.

A fixed mindset is one that believes the person cannot move forward, cannot do things in a new or different way. They perceive themselves as stuck or trapped, helpless and dependent on someone else for everything they need.

Rescue Rebuild Restore

I have a growth mindset about myself. I love to learn and study, read books and seek out trainings, and certifications. However, for someone else, I might perceive them as incapable of learning new things. My belief that this young mom, for example, is going to stay stuck in a perpetual cycle of drugs, domestic violence, and abandonment will cause me to respond to her needs in ways that could reinforce the very negative behaviors that I would love to see halted in her life.

I may communicate that I don't trust her to make good decisions by making decisions for her, rather than giving her an opportunity to express her own thoughts or opinions. I may brush off her desires for friendship because I assume she will just use me, that she will try to manipulate me and take advantage of me. So, my subconscious response to her may be to build a protective wall around my heart. I may even claim it is "setting a healthy boundary."

But what she perceives is that I don't actually care, I won't listen to the root issues of her heart. I'm a liar and I don't love her. I can't be trusted and she is still alone in her life of trauma, abuse, and pain.

My belief in the other person's capacity to learn and grow will directly affect how I treat them. And they will know exactly what I think, whether I realize it or not.

Unfortunately you can't control whether someone has a fixed or growth mindset about themselves. You can only control *your* beliefs and perceptions about *them*. Situations may seem grim but I believe that "if there is still breath then there is still hope." The Lord can and will transform life, where He is permitted to work. And again, that's not a decision you get to make. Your responsibility is merely to meet needs and point toward Jesus.

However, you *can* give opportunities for people to discover growth within themselves. And we're going to talk more about that in Chapter 8.

B.   The Receivers

Put yourself in their shoes for a moment, the shoes of the typical receiver.

Think about their perspective, arriving at ministry after ministry, sitting through intrusive questions, inadequate programs, and unrealistic expectations, all while hoping to get the help they know they need but cannot attain on their own.

By the time they arrive at your church ministry doors, asking for help has probably become a common pattern of solving the problem of their survival. Do they need food? There's an agency or church benevolence program for that. Do they need clothes? Someone is bound to feel enough pity to rifle through their closet for ill-fitting castoffs. Do they need money or a bill paid? There is always a reason why they can't afford it themselves. And, generally, the story needs to be good enough, serious enough to justify the dollar amount they are requesting.

Chronic receivers are accustomed to stretching the truth as far as they need to in order to tug a giver's heart strings *enough* to get the help the receiver needs. Manipulation is a survival tactic.

I'll say that again: manipulation is a survival tactic. It's frustrating and hurtful for the giver to recognize they're being manipulated but nevertheless, it's a useful survival tool in the toolbox of virtually every chronic receiver.

Before you get too upset about it, remember the road that the receiver is walking…

The reason a person develops a fixed mindset in the first place is because they do not see themselves as having learned, changed, grown, or become better or wiser in the past, therefore they don't see potential for learning in their future. They have been conditioned, often from an early age, to believe they are worthless, hopeless, stupid, that they deserve the consequences of their actions and they have failed over and over and over. These false beliefs are deeply ingrained and difficult to challenge. We'll talk about exactly how you can challenge others toward a growth mindset in Chapter 8.

Self-Assessment: Examining Your Mindset About Receivers

Use this assessment to reflect on your beliefs and expectations about receivers. Rate each statement on a scale of 1-5 (1 = Strongly Disagree, 5 = Strongly Agree). Total your score to assess your mindset and identify opportunities for growth.

- I believe most receivers are capable of change and growth, even if their progress is slow or challenging.
- I sometimes see receivers as helpless or stuck, assuming they can't overcome their circumstances.
- I trust God to transform receivers' lives, even when their behaviors (like manipulation) frustrate me.
- I offer opportunities for receivers to grow (e.g., classes, job training) and celebrate their progress, no matter how small.
- I recognize that receivers' fixed mindsets (e.g., hopelessness, inferiority) stem from trauma, poverty, or addiction, not personal failure.

- I pray for God's vision to see receivers' potential, rather than focusing on their current struggles.

- I build trust-based relationships with receivers, even if it takes time and patience, to help them discover self-efficacy.

- I avoid making decisions for receivers, instead empowering them to express their own needs and goals.

- I feel hopeful about receivers' futures, trusting that "if there is still breath, there is still hope" in Christ.

Scoring:

- 9-18: You may need to shift toward a growth mindset, seeking God's perspective to see receivers' potential and serve with hope.

- 19-36: You're developing a balanced mindset, but there's room to deepen your trust in God's transformative power.

- 37-45: Your growth mindset is strong and faith-filled, but continue seeking His wisdom to sustain your ministry.

Now What?

So what can you *actually* do about it? While you can't directly affect their ability to see themselves growing, you *can* present opportunities for them to grow. And then, you can kindly point their progress out to them, when they become frustrated or disappointed in themselves.

While we can't directly change a receiver's mindset, we can offer opportunities for growth, point them toward Jesus, and walk alongside them with love and wisdom. True change will cost us—time, care, effort, and vulnerability—but their restoration is worth it. As we serve, we trust the Lord to transform lives, rebuild hope, and restore dignity, one unique heart at a time, whether they are giving or receiving.

Self-efficacy is what you're impacting—a person's sense of self-worth that is rooted in evidence. Self-*esteem* tends to be externally driven, but self-*worth* is rooted internally.

These opportunities for growth and learning could come in the form of classes, case management, job-training opportunities, and other activities. In order to affect their sense of self-efficacy, you must build a <u>trust-based relationship.</u> Expect that to take time and patience on your part. We'll talk more about that soon.

Effecting true change in another person is going to cost you far more than you may yet realize. There is a price to be paid—in time, care, money, and effort. Their soul hangs in the balance and is absolutely worth your efforts. But you have to be prepared, eyes wide open, for the true cost or else you risk giving up too soon.

In the chapters ahead, we'll explore practical steps to implement the RRR Framework, fostering growth, healing poverty mindsets, addressing trauma, overcoming addiction, and supporting mental health—all with the rugged individualism and realistic goals we've discussed. For now, let us pray for the courage to see, love, and serve as Jesus does, bridging the gap between givers and receivers with grace.

Chapter 4: Counting the Cost, Love Never Fails

As followers of Christ, we are called to love the least of these with unwavering compassion, wisdom, and sacrifice—rooted in the unconditional, Biblical love that reflects God's heart. In the RRR framework, this love is the secret key that unlocks everything we do, enabling us to rescue, rebuild, and restore with grace. Unconditional, Biblical

> **Stephan Friedrich**
> @s_stephanf
>
> Why do many children in #fostercare seem so intolerant to a safe, loving home?
> You know when you run a nice warm bath but you're really cold, and it feels like it's burning your legs so you can't get in? That's how love feels for someone who has never known it.

love is way more powerful than anything we could ever create from within ourselves.

When I teach the RRR Method, there's a great meme that I love to use.

This, right here, ladies and gentlemen.

This is the challenge you face with every new receiver you meet. We humans were all built to crave love. Love from our Creator, love from one another.

And yet, so few of us understand what *unconditional* love actually looks like. "Love" is too often the transactional, manipulative language that abusers use to get their way. "Love" has often been the language of forced obedience and submission rather than a mutual connection, rooted in trust and acceptance.

Boyfriends tell girls that they love them—only to leave when they've gotten all they want out of her, leaving her broken, hurting, pregnant, and alone.

Parents tell children they love them—while abusing their position of authority so badly that children turn to drugs, alcohol, or self-harm to mask the pain the parents' "love" leaves behind. This counterfeit love leaves receivers skeptical, fearful, and resistant, as if a warm, safe embrace feels like a burning pain to someone who's never known true care.

What does *unconditional* love look like?

Let's walk through what is probably a very familiar passage of Scripture, 1 Corinthians 13:3-8, using *The Passion Translation*.

And if I were to be so generous as to give away everything I owned to feed the poor, and to offer my body to be burned as a martyr, without the pure motive of love, I would gain nothing of value. Verse 3

Rescue Rebuild Restore

How pure is your motive to love the least of these, those who need your help more than you need them? As givers, we hold a position of power and authority, sometimes even life and death (literally or figuratively). Are you wielding that power in grace, gentleness, and long-suffering, or in frustration, disappointment, and unrealistic expectations?

Love is large and incredibly patient. Love is gentle and consistently kind to all. It refuses to be jealous when blessing comes to someone else. Love does not brag about one's achievements nor inflate its own importance. Verse 4

The first statement, in the original Aramaic, could also be translated as "Love patiently endures mistreatment." Love needs to be incredibly patient, remaining steadfast even in difficult situations, especially with those shaped by trauma, addiction, or chronic poverty.

Love does not traffic in shame and disrespect, nor selfishly seek its own honor. Love is not quickly irritated or quick to take offense. Verse 5

How are you documenting your work as a giver?

Think about those pictures you often see on social media, of someone giving money or a bottle of water to someone in need. Clean, well-dressed smiling faces next to someone who is dirty, downcast, uncomfortable. A great photo op for one person is a shame-filled demonstration of another's desperate lack. Are you (accidentally) using their shame and hopelessness as a steppingstone to help you demonstrate how kind, thoughtful, and caring you are? Love doesn't need likes and shares. Love doesn't need anyone to know what you're doing.

Love covers over shame and inadequacy and dirt and body odor, offering shelter rather than exposure.

How do you respond when receivers are angry or disappointed? When you have to turn someone away or say no to a request, how does the receiver's attitude affect yours?

Love joyfully celebrates honesty (or "reality" or "truth") *and finds no delight in what is wrong* (or "injustice" or "unrighteousness"). Verse 6

Receivers often face systemic injustice—wrongful imprisonment, broken promises, or cascading consequences from minor setbacks. Love acknowledges this reality, standing against unrighteousness while celebrating truth, even when their stories challenge us. It is incredibly important that you understand that the lower a person falls, the greater society works against them.

Ask your receivers to share their story and you'll often hear tales of injustice from people and institutions of authority. Wrongful imprisonment, harmful accusations, promises unfulfilled, theft and abuse of power frequently play into the stories of many receivers.

A simple case of missing a court date can trigger a series of events whereby a person is stopped on a routine traffic violation, arrested on the spot (because of a bench warrant issued due to the missed court appearance), car is impounded, kids (in the backseat) are now in foster care, a good job is lost (due to being in jail and not at work), and now rent can't be paid so the family is also evicted.

That's a true story, lived out by more than one of our clients. There is an injustice to living very close to the edge of desperation. Seemingly minor inconvenience becomes the catalyst for severe repercussions, sometimes impossible to overcome.

Rescue Rebuild Restore

Your receivers are often already living a life of injustice and oppression, even before taking into consideration their skin color, accent, gender, or sexual orientation.

Their assertion that their problems are someone else's fault is not entirely wrong. That's not to say the receiver standing in front of you hasn't had a role to play, contributing to their own circumstances. Very few people are *truly* fully innocent, but nevertheless, they are often *also* the victims of an unjust world, organized to keep them trapped in despair and lack.

From obstacles around housing, to loss of employment to drugs and addiction, to mental health and a social safety net that spends more time <u>hindering</u> rather than <u>helping</u> people move up the social ladder, injustice is a common theme in many of their stories.

Love is a safe place of shelter, for it never stops believing the best for others. Love never takes failure as defeat, for it never gives up. Verse 7

Is your program a safe place? Are *you* a safe person? The word translated here as "shelter" (*stego*) would actually be more accurate as "roof." Love protects, believes in potential, and persists, even when receivers relapse into addiction, return to harmful patterns, or leave your care.

Now, I'm going to assume that you consider yourself and your ministry as "safe." I imagine there are very few people, especially those reading this book, who would *not* consider themselves safe. However, we will examine, in Part 3, what a safe space actually is, from the receiver's perspective rather than the giver's. Then, we'll discuss ways you can ensure that every receiver *feels* safe with you.

Love never stops loving. Verse 8a

The Passion Translation has a beautiful note about the original Aramaic translation of "Love never stops loving." This could also be translated as, "Love never, not even once, fails (lapses)" or "Love never falls down (it keeps going higher)."

Say what you want about TPT, that's beautiful right there. That's what it's all about. That's what our beloved receivers need—unconditional, unfailing love.

Not that I'm saying unconditional *approval* of harmful actions, behaviors or attitudes. Unconditional love of the person in front of you does *not* mean unconditional acceptance of their addiction, their abuse, their fears, their codependency.

It merely means loving them as Christ loves them. Love them as Christ loves you—patiently, gently, with eyes wide open to their true nature and also to their great potential to be "transformed more fully into the image of Christ."

Count the Cost

We in the Church often talk about unconditional love. But do we do it? We love to hear how God loves *us* unconditionally, but do we actually do the same toward others? What does loving someone unconditionally actually look like, on a daily basis?

Before we can really dive into what it looks like, we need to consider its price. The thing about unconditional love is that it's quite expensive.

Think "pouring out an alabaster box of costly perfume on the feet of Jesus and wiping it off with your hair" expensive.

Just like with any relationship, there's a cost—a cost of time, effort, and resources.

Rescue Rebuild Restore

In Luke 14, Jesus gives us a pair of parables to help us understand the cost of being a disciple of Jesus. But I think that this principle of counting the cost applies much more broadly.

Let's look at these verses and you'll see what I mean.

And whoever does not carry their cross and follow Me cannot be My disciple.

Suppose one of you wants to build a tower. Won't you first sit down and estimate the cost to see if you have enough money to complete it? For if you lay the foundation and are not able to finish it, everyone who sees it will ridicule you, saying, "This person began to build and wasn't able to finish."

Or suppose a king is about to go to war against another king. Won't he first sit down and consider whether he is able with 10,000 men to oppose the one coming against him with 20,000? If he is not able, he will send a delegation while the other is still a long way off and will ask for terms of peace.

In the same way, those of you who do not give up everything you have cannot be My disciples.

Luke 14:27-33

The concept of counting the cost is usually taught from the perspective of following Jesus. But I want to use it here with the picture of *serving* Jesus. I regularly teach this concept to our new volunteers as well as ministry leaders across the country.

Proverbs 8 goes into beautiful detail about Wisdom. And what I love about this understanding of creation is that God Himself laid out the blueprint for all of creation, all the way to the end of eternity, which Scripture tells us He holds in the palm of His hand. And then He began building, brick by brick, the foundations of the world that we see in Genesis.

He had the luxury of seeing all of the costs that would be required and he deemed it worth paying.

We humans, however, do not have the luxury of knowing, in advance, 100% of the price of anything that we do.

If you've ever remodeled your kitchen or built a house from the ground up, you know that the price the general contractor quotes you before the project begins is rarely the same price that you actually end up paying, once everything is fully complete.

Whether you discover drywall is on backorder or you need to hire a different plumber, who costs more, or you simply want to go with a different backsplash or kitchen tile, prices change. Plans change.

The same principle applies with our work with other people. You may be working with someone who was recently incarcerated, and suddenly you discover that they were actually in prison for sex crimes toward children. The cost has changed.

The single mom that you so generously moved into your basement apartment now wants to move her boyfriend in as well. The cost has changed.

The homeless veteran that you have been working with suddenly shows up at your church, drunk or high or both. The price that you pay to continue serving has suddenly gone up.

The idea that we can count the cost one time and be willing to pay it 100% of the time in the future is foolish. That is simply not how it works in our world. We cannot know the full cost in advance, so we have to be willing to recalculate whether or not we will pay the revised price.

Every time a new client comes in, there is a new cost that must be paid. And your volunteers have to choose to continue paying that price.

Let me give you an example of this, from my own ministry.

A couple of years ago, a young pregnant woman was released from jail four days before Christmas. Jamie came into our home and gave birth mid February. She was doing well in our classes and in the job training program, however we knew she was still struggling.

Many of our moms struggle for a long time. Lasting life change is hard and requires both patience and sacrifice, that whole "dying to self" thing.

She was a sweet girl and had endeared herself to several of our volunteers. So everyone was excited when Jamie had saved enough money to buy a car, shortly after her daughter was born.

You want to know the first place she went after she finished working, on her very first day of freedom with her new car and her infant daughter?

Straight to her old trap house (drug house) and she shot up with fentanyl. With her daughter in the car seat on the floor of the trap house.

Yeah, that was a hard one for staff and volunteers alike. Contrary to what you're probably assuming, we didn't kick her out of the program. We locked down (metaphorically speaking). We knew that, for her to have been clean for the four-ish months she'd been with us, and then six months in jail before that, and then for her very first act to be *fentanyl*... this was incredibly important. We locked everything down, pulled her back to Phase 1 status. Talked with her in depth, tried to get her to go into rehab...

Her actions even scared *her*, especially as she thought of what could have happened to her beautiful little daughter.

Despite everything we tried, however, Jamie left us within a few weeks. Last I heard, the baby is in foster care and Mom is in jail.

Now, that whole situation was incredibly difficult for us staff. But we also have a deep level of trauma training and a lot of experience with these situations. The volunteers? Oh they grieved. One of my board members, who had been leading a Bible study with the girls, would drive around town looking for Jamie's car, praying to locate her.

The emotional toll it took on our volunteers and the other clients cannot be overstated. Everyone grieved but there were a couple volunteers who simply could not continue working with us. They could not envision themselves opening up their hearts to another client, and risking that level of grief, pain, and heartbreak.

They counted the cost and discovered the price that they had paid was too high. They were not willing to pay it again.

Unconditional love is extremely costly, which is why it is so rare, especially in the circles that our clients have traveled in.

As you build programs to love "the least of these" wisely, remember the high price of loving well. It will take a toll, not only on you and your trained team, but also on the other clients as well.

The clients grieved too. They grieved for their friend. They grieved for her daughter. But they also grieved afresh for themselves. They had to acknowledge that they could also choose a similar path. Would they choose wisely? There's a certain amount of both fear and survivor's guilt at play here.

The girls would alternately text her, checking in, asking her to come back, and also asking staff if she would be allowed back. Would redemption be possible for her, while also wondering if it would be available for themselves? Would they fall or would they succeed?

We did our best to assure everyone that, yes, second chances are possible but also, that's something Jamie would have to actually want. We're not in the business of kidnapping our mamas and forcing them clean. That doesn't work.

Every time one of our clients leaves too early, we all grieve, including the clients. But when it happens in such a scary and dramatic fashion, there's an added layer of fear for themselves and their own shaky sobriety in addition to their fear and grief for their friend.

Unconditional love requires time, effort, resources, and emotional sacrifice. It takes a toll on you, your team, and your clients, especially when they grieve a friend's relapse or fear their own fragility.

But as Proverbs 8 reminds us, God Himself counted the cost of creation, deeming it worth paying. Are you willing to recalculate and pay the price, even when costs rise? Is she—or he—still worth it, despite addiction, trauma, poverty, or mental health struggles?

Only you, in prayer and partnership with God, can decide.

Self-Assessment: Evaluating Your Commitment to Unconditional Love

Use this assessment to reflect on your readiness to love unconditionally. Rate each statement on a scale of 1-5 (1 = Strongly Disagree, 5 = Strongly Agree). Total your score to gauge your commitment and identify areas for growth.

- I am willing to love receivers unconditionally, even when they relapse, leave, or behave in ways that hurt me.

- I regularly pray for God's strength to pay the high cost of loving others, including time, effort, and emotional sacrifice.

- I recognize that my love for receivers must be free of judgment, shame, or unrealistic expectations, mirroring Christ's love.

- I trust God to transform receivers' lives, even when their progress is slow or they face setbacks like addiction or trauma.

- I am prepared to recalculate the cost of loving well, accepting that it may rise with new challenges or disappointments.

- I create a safe, sheltering environment for receivers, protecting them from shame and believing the best for them.

- I avoid seeking recognition or praise for my giving, focusing instead on loving quietly as Jesus did.

- I feel hopeful and patient when receivers struggle, trusting that "love never fails" (1 Corinthians 13:8).

- I am willing to grieve with my team and clients when a receiver's journey takes a painful turn, like Jamie's story.

Scoring:

- 9-18: You may need to deepen your commitment to unconditional love, seeking God's guidance to endure its cost.

- 19-36: You're on a good path, but there's room to strengthen your resolve, trusting God's provision through challenges.

- 37-45: Your commitment to unconditional love is strong and faith-filled, but continue seeking His wisdom to sustain it.

Chapter 5: The Catch

As followers of Christ, we are called to love the least of these with wisdom, compassion, and discernment—avoiding pitfalls that hinder true restoration. In the RRR framework, understanding why common approaches to serving often fail is crucial to building effective, individualized programs.

Let's examine three pervasive myths that many organizations and individuals fall into when helping those in need, rooted in poverty, trauma, addiction, and mental health challenges. Let us prayerfully explore these myths, trusting God to guide us toward wiser, more loving responses.

Too often, well-meaning givers—churches, ministries, and individuals—rely on approaches that seem logical but fail to address the deep, unique needs of receivers. These myths, shaped by our human tendencies and lack of knowledge, can perpetuate harm rather than healing. Let's uncover them and seek God's wisdom to respond differently.

Myth #1: Better Rules Will Fix the Problem

When things go wrong, our first instinct is often to create new rules—adding questions to intake forms, tightening policies, or setting stricter boundaries to protect ourselves. We think, "If only we had one more rule, we'd be safe." But this rarely works. The issue isn't always the rules; it's our understanding of the people we serve.

When we grasp the motives, behavioral patterns, and brain science behind why receivers act as they do—particularly through the lens of trauma, addiction, poverty, and mental health—we can better understand the "logic" behind their actions or attitudes. As Chapter 6 will reveal, chronic trauma activates the sympathetic nervous system (survival mode), driving behaviors like manipulation or resistance to rules, while poverty mindsets or addiction coping mechanisms create patterns of need that rules alone can't address.

In our early ministry days, we updated intake forms and policies with every new client or departure, only to find that each rule created more harm than good. Rules made for our convenience—such as limiting dollar amounts per client, banning certain diagnoses or medications, or prohibiting cigarettes—often clashed with the individualized needs of receivers. We learned that rigid rules can alienate those we serve, reinforcing their sense of helplessness or mistrust.

Rules are essential guardrails, keeping everyone safe and clarifying boundaries, but they must be trauma-informed and flexible, tailored to each person's story. As Proverbs 19:2 warns, "Desire without knowledge is not good—how much more will hasty feet miss the way!" We'll explore what makes a "good" rule in later chapters, but for now, let's shift from reacting with more rules to responding with understanding and grace.

We've learned so much the hard way, and I want to help you avoid that learning curve as much as I can. In the Resources

Section at the end of this book, you'll find a Trauma-Informed vs. Traditional Organization cheat sheet which will help you recognize the differences in responses. and hopefully, this will help you develop more effective rules and policies.

Myth #1b: Well, Just Leave Then

A related trap, often born of frustration or fear, is believing a receiver is "broken beyond repair" or "unfixable," leading us to remove them from our programs prematurely. We think, "It's not our rules or approach that's the problem—it's them." This sentiment is harmful because it mirrors what receivers have experienced throughout their lives—rejection and abandonment, especially in the context of trauma or addiction.

Instead of expelling them, we can ask, "Why do they resist this rule or behave this way?" Their perspective often reveals valid insights—rooted in survival tactics, injustice, or misunderstanding. Like teenagers, receivers may push back against "because I said so," but explaining a rule's purpose can build trust, even if they don't agree. More often, their reasoning makes sense, offering a chance to teach and learn together. Kicking someone out too early stems from our fear, arrogance, or lack of understanding, but God calls us to do things differently, as 1 Peter 4:8 urges: "Above all, love each other deeply, because love covers over a multitude of sins."

Myth #2: They Just Need More Help

Another common trap is believing that more help—more money, resources, or support—will move receivers forward. Kindhearted volunteers might cosign for a vehicle, move someone into their basement, or pay for car repairs, thinking,

"If I just give more, they'll achieve stability." While giving is not inherently wrong, this approach often fails because receivers may not learn to value or maintain what they receive, especially if shaped by a transient, "easy come, easy go" lifestyle rooted in poverty or trauma.

As Chapter 7 highlights, receivers with a poverty mindset or addiction struggles may not see long-term value in material help, selling or losing items like furniture or appliances when times get hard. Concepts like "learned helplessness" and "entitlement mentality" emerge here—patterns where receivers, conditioned by chronic lack or trauma, come to expect help without taking responsibility, or feel unable to change their circumstances. Our role isn't to fill every gap or achieve full independence for them, but to partner with God and each receiver, fostering growth through realistic, individualized goals.

Jesus modeled this in John 5:6-8, asking the paralyzed man, "Do you want to get well?" before healing him—inviting action, not just providing. We must ask similar questions, ensuring our help empowers, not enables, trusting the Lord to transform their hearts and habits.

Myth #3: I Know What They Need *or* I Can Handle It

Perhaps the most dangerous myth is the belief that we, as givers, know what receivers need without asking, or that we can handle any situation on our own. This savior mentality—swooping in like a hero to "save the day"—can undermine receivers' ability to act for themselves and lead us into situations we are unprepared for, physically, emotionally, or spiritually.

Crossing hidden lines—whether through over-involvement or pride—can result in harm: givers have faced violence, and receivers have been hurt so deeply they never seek help again. As Scripture warns in Proverbs 16:18, "Pride goes before destruction, a haughty spirit before a fall." We are not anyone's savior—only Jesus holds that role. Our calling is to walk alongside receivers, listening to their stories, understanding their trauma, addiction, poverty, or mental health struggles, and partnering with professionals and God's wisdom, not acting as lone heroes.

This myth reflects arrogance or fear, as seen in Myth #1b above, but it's rooted in a lack of humility. We must recognize our limits, seek God's guidance, and trust Him to do what we cannot, ensuring our love is wise and safe for all.

Moving Forward in Wisdom

These myths trap us because they prioritize our convenience, pride, or assumptions over the real needs of receivers. But as we serve, we must trust God to guide us beyond quick fixes, seeking understanding of their poverty mindsets, trauma responses, addiction struggles, and mental health challenges.

In the chapters ahead, we'll explore trauma-informed rules, realistic goals, and safe, transformative programs, building on the rugged individualism and unconditional love we've discussed. For now, let us pray for the humility to listen, the patience to learn, and the faith to love wisely.

Self-Assessment: Uncovering Your Approach to Serving

Use this assessment to reflect on your response to the myths in this chapter. Rate each statement on a scale of 1-5 (1 =

Strongly Disagree, 5 = Strongly Agree). Total your score to evaluate your approach and identify areas for growth.

- I often create or rely on new rules to protect myself or my ministry when challenges arise with receivers.
- I believe that giving more help (money, resources, etc.) will solve a receiver's problems, even if they don't take responsibility.
- I sometimes think I know what receivers need without asking their perspective, acting as their "savior" instead of partner.
- I've considered removing a receiver from our program because I felt they were "unfixable" or too difficult, rather than seeking understanding.
- I regularly pray for God's wisdom to understand the motives and behaviors of receivers, especially in light of trauma, poverty, or addiction.
- I check my pride or fear, ensuring I don't impose my assumptions on receivers but listen to their stories and needs.
- I trust God to transform receivers' lives, even when their progress is slow or they resist rules or help.
- I partner with professionals or seek training to better handle complex situations like mental health or addiction, rather than acting alone.
- I create flexible, trauma-informed rules that prioritize receivers' needs over my convenience, fostering trust and growth.

Scoring:

- 9-18: You may be relying on these myths, needing to seek God's guidance to serve with humility and understanding.

- 19-36: You're making progress, but there's room to refine your approach, focusing on partnership and wisdom over quick fixes.

- 37-45: Your approach is aligned with God's heart, but continue seeking His wisdom to sustain your ministry effectively.

Part 2: Rescue, Rebuild, Restore

Chapter 6: Wisdom to Understand

"Wisdom has built her house. She has hewn its seven pillars."
Proverbs 9:1

In Chapter 4, we talked about unconditional love and how necessary it is to help "the least of these" move from a place of shame and hopelessness to a place of stability and grace.

But there's another aspect to unconditional love that we need to discuss right here.

Wisdom. Rooted in knowledge and experience, wisdom is the way in which you live out unconditional love in practical ways. Wisdom is how you help without hurting, to borrow the phrase from my buddies at the Chalmers Center.

Proverbs 8 is one of my favorite chapters in the Bible. It paints a beautiful picture of God using the tool of Wisdom to craft our world. I picture her as the paintbrush Jesus used to bring to life the words God the Father speaks. This kind of Wisdom comes from God alone, a supernatural creative force.

Earthly wisdom is knowledge gained through experience, especially from failures that you've learned from.

You need both types of wisdom, supernatural and earthly, in order to express unconditional love to others in a way that is helpful and not harmful—to yourself and to them.

The nice thing about earthly wisdom is that you don't need to have personally experienced the failures and self-reflection which lead to wisdom. Learning wisdom from the stories and testimonies of others can be just as effective.

So let me share a few things that will help you understand why our clients act, think and behave the way that they do.

The Long-Lasting Effects of Trauma, Abuse, and Addiction

This is usually the place where you would expect that I'd start telling you how to accomplish powerful, lasting, life transformations in the clients you serve, by following some exact steps...

Unfortunately, it's not that simple. What I offer you is a series of principles which create the trauma-informed lens through which you'll see each of your clients in a new way.

Much like the various lenses at the optometrist's office, I'll help you see more clearly, more deeply, more completely. And then, in Part 3, I'll help you craft a new way forward which meets each person where they are and enables you to build relationship bridges toward a future of sustainable stability.

These lenses are:
1. Poverty Mindset
2. Trauma
3. Addiction
4. Mental Health

Once you begin to view each of your clients through their appropriate lens (or lenses), everything becomes more clear, more manageable, and less scary.

Lens One – Poverty Mindset

This was the first lens the Lord taught me, so I feel like it's the optimal place to start. The lens of poverty has three dimensions:

- Material poverty (lack of resources),
- Poverty mindset (a worldview, perspective) and
- Chronic poverty culture (where both physical lack and a worldview of lack affect a group of people).

Think of these three aspects as varying thicknesses of the lens of poverty. (I'm gonna milk this analogy as much as possible!)

A. <u>Material Poverty</u>

This is likely the one you're most familiar with. Most people immediately assume "lack of money" when they think of the materially poor, but that's only one aspect.

A lack of resources can also include lack of employment opportunities, lack of educational opportunities, lack of healthy relationships (due to high crime, high violence lifestyles).

For example, one area where you may see a lack of resources in a client is in employment. Sometimes, it really does take an inside relationship to get hired at a certain company. It can definitely be about "who you know," and our clients generally don't know people who would be useful to help them locate a good-paying job, purchase a reliable, affordable, used vehicle, or find an opening in a local daycare.

Everything is made harder for them because of their lack of useful connections.

   B. <u>Poverty Mindset</u>

Poverty mindset, poverty thinking, orphan mindset can all be used to mean the same thing. This is a worldview in which, as people look around themselves, all they see is lack. They don't recognize opportunities or resources available to them. And this, of course, relates back to our discussion of growth versus fixed mindset, back in Chapter 3.

It's separate and distinct from material poverty because you can actually be quite wealthy and still have a poverty mindset. Similarly, you can live in desperately poor circumstances and yet *not* have a poverty mindset. You can recognize the resources around you and eventually go on to accomplish great things.

"I don't have anyone to help me" could be accurate, OR perhaps there's a disconnect in who they actually know, who may be able to help them. It could be that there is a relationship which was damaged, and needs mending, or the client is making assumptions about whether an acquaintance would be willing to help your client accomplish a task. For many of our clients, they have gone back to the same people within their family or friend group so often, usually asking for money, that they've exhausted the goodwill of others.

Your client may perceive these relationships as burned beyond repair, but that may not be the case, especially when they begin making progress toward stability and their family and friends begin to see true change emerging.

C. <u>Chronic Poverty Culture</u>

You can probably guess where I'm going with this one. When people live in a community where there are few resources (think food deserts, medical deserts, employment deserts), poverty mindset becomes entrenched into a subcultural belief that this is "how we live, this is who we are."

Have you ever heard the saying, "Three Generations to Failure but Seven to Success"? Here's how that works: An individual can be born into a middle-class lifestyle, raised with a middle-class mindset, and then live in material poverty without being affected by poverty mindset. But then their children learn both from their parents (resource mindset) and the community around them (poverty culture). And now the grandchildren are fed a higher dose of poverty thinking and observe the poverty culture around them. Resource mindset begins to fade with each successive generation.

There are always outliers, individuals who gravitate to resources and opportunities, but the vast majority don't. And then, in the opposite direction, it takes several generations of hard work and intentional effort to build a legacy of both resources *and* resource thinking.

In this Hidden Rules of Poverty diagram, (Ruby Payne), you can see how the three classes tend to view the world around them so differently.

	Poverty	**Middle Class**	**Wealth**
Driving Forces	Relationships, survival, entertainment	Achievement, work	Financial, political, social connections

Possessions	People	Things	One-of-a-kind, legacies
Money	To be used, spent	To be managed	To be conserved, invested
Food	Did you have enough? Quantity	Did you like it? Quality	How did it look? Presentation
Time	Present is most important. Decisions based on feelings or survival.	Future is most important. Decisions based on future ramifications.	Traditions and history are most important. Decisions influenced by decorum and family status.

This is usually the place, in a live training, where I pause and ask, "Thoughts, questions, comments?" It's a lot to consider.

Far too many of us in the helping field are what I term "fixers." We're naturally looking for solutions and it can confuse and frustrate us when others either don't see solutions for themselves or don't act on our suggestions. (That is literally why I ended up *not* becoming a therapist—they don't actually *have to* do what I said!)

And yet, as we reflect on what kind of environment these people we serve were raised in, both what they were taught and what they observed, it is much easier to understand why she expects a new package of diapers or a new bottle of prenatal vitamins every time she comes to your class. Or why he assumes you'll give him a ride or a few dollars every time you see him.

How will an understanding of poverty mindset and chronic poverty culture affect how you work with clients in the future? I could literally write a whole 'nother book on that one question...

A better question, for right now: How does this information affect how you view the people you serve right now? What observations stand out to you immediately, after reading this section?

Email me! I want to know! suzanne@becharitywise.com

Lens Two – Trauma's Effects on Brain Development

I started this whole journey by volunteering at a pregnancy resource center for seven years before opening Foundation House. I'd also experienced my own traumatic situations before that, so I wasn't surprised by the fact that these women moving into our home had experienced trauma.

What *did* surprise me, back in the beginning, was that simply removing them from their traumatic environment *was not enough*. When I began learning about the lasting effects of trauma on our brains and our bodies, I was absolutely floored by the information I'm about to share with you.

Trauma is something that nearly every person will experience in their lifetimes. We humans invariably experience some type of traumatic event, whether it be a car accident, a cancer diagnosis, an abusive relationship, or another type of dangerous situation.

Trauma is not the thing that happened; that's the traumatic *event*. Trauma is the *effect* of that event on you, afterwards, which is why one person can be so deeply affected by an event while someone else seems to take it all in stride.

Our bodies were created with a beautiful system for emergency management: the Autonomic Nervous System (ANS). When this system works well, it enables our bodies to move into protective measures against the traumatic event. Whether we are taking evasive action or freezing in position, this system sets off the emergency warning signals in our brains which trigger our body's instinctive protective response to unknown or dangerous situations.

Autonomic Nervous System

This system is composed of two parts, the Sympathetic and the Parasympathetic Systems.

AUTONOMIC NERVOUS SYSTEM

SYMPATHETIC (HOT) SYSTEM	PARASYMPATHETIC (COOL) SYSTEM
• Accelerates heart rate	• Promotes digestion
• Constricts blood vessels	• Intestinal motility
• Raises blood pressure, muscle tension, physical sensations amplified	• Fuel storage (increases insulin activity)
• Inhibition of insulin production, to maximize fuel availability	• Resistance to infection
	• Circulation to non-vital organs
• Cold hands and feet	• Releases endorphins
• Headaches	• Decreases heart rate, blood pressure, and body temperature

Imagine you are eating lunch in the park on your break from work. You've just finished eating your sandwich and chips and are cleaning up your mess. You are preparing to head back to your car and return to work when suddenly, in the distance, you hear a pack of angry, yelping dogs heading your direction. Instantly, your body shifts its attention from gently digesting your sandwich to suddenly increasing blood flow to your legs so that you can run away.

This is the Sympathetic System in action. Frequently referred to as the "Hot" system, it accelerates your heart rate, constricts blood vessels, raises things like blood pressure and muscle tension, and amplifies physical sensations. All for the express purpose of ensuring that your body is as equipped as possible for the fight-flight-freeze response that it anticipates.

The Parasympathetic system, or "Cool" system, is the one that most people are in, most of the time. This system promotes digestion and circulation. It maintains heart rate, blood pressure, and body temperature within a normal range.

Your body tells your brain what is happening, your brain makes a quick decision and tells your body how to respond, and your body reports back to your brain on how effective its directions were. Then your body and brain will repeat that process until you're safe.

When these two systems are out of balance, the body responds with survival strategies at the expense of intentionality, deliberateness, and integrity.

The sympathetic nervous system is perfectly designed to send the body into survival mode. It is excellent at its job… unless one's lifestyle is that of frequent chaos, like many clients we see.

Neurobiology of Trauma

When the brain receives the notification from your body, from the Sympathetic system, that danger is imminent, the brain moves into action—releasing hormone chemicals which communicate with the various parts of the body, causing the physical responses listed above.

This chemical cocktail acts as a signal to the rest of the body to shut down non-emergency systems and shift its attention to survival.

Yes, like on Star Trek, when the enemy ship is closing in and Captain Picard (or Kirk!) says to turn off all non-essential systems and send the extra power to shields, or to warp speed. That's exactly what her body is doing when it shuts down digestion or emotion regulation or the assignment you literally *just* gave her.

Survival.

These chemicals take about 18-24 hours to be reabsorbed into the body after they are released. When the body releases this emergency cocktail, it is always the same dose. According to Dr. Louis Cozolino (2011), these chemicals are catabolic, which means that they break down protein and stop protein synthesis, eating away at existing brain tissue.

In an emergency situation, this would be considered acceptable loss of function. Just like when you are trying to escape quickly from a dangerous situation, your stomach doesn't need to worry about adequate digestion, your brain doesn't need to continue processing new information. It only needs to help you escape. All other processes can be resumed later once the emergency has passed.

Imagine, however, that your life is so chaotic that you are constantly bombarded with emergency messages. You are homeless or in an abusive situation. Or both. Everywhere you turn, you are met with crisis after crisis. If your body consistently releases dose after dose of this emergency cocktail, the very chemicals that are designed to help you shut down non-emergency systems begin to damage the brain, sometimes beyond repair.

Herein lies the true issue…

This system was designed for emergencies, not for daily life. How many of our clients have lived 18-24 hours without another dosage?

It may be surprising, but it's not wrong to say that your clients' brains have been <u>damaged</u> due to their trauma histories.

Think about that for a minute.

Doesn't that alone help you offer more grace, patience, and understanding to your clients?

While these are lasting changes, our brains were so cleverly designed (yay God!) that we can absolutely repair and rewire them. It just takes time, effort, and understanding the process—which is exactly what we teach you in the **Rescue, Rebuild, Restore Framework.**

Adverse Childhood Experiences

Now let's think about the childhood that many of your clients likely experienced. Think about a child experiencing these traumatic situations over and over. Think of the destructive nature of these chemicals in the developing brain.

This gives you a bit of an insight into the <u>lasting impact</u> of Adverse Childhood Experiences.

Adverse Childhood Experiences (ACEs) is a 10-question assessment tool, developed by the US Centers for Disease Control and Prevention (CDC) and Kaiser Permanente, which examines an individual's personal history, looking for instances of adverse experiences.

The prevalence of ACEs is strongly correlated to the development and severity of a wide range of health problems throughout a person's lifespan. ACEs include: physical abuse, sexual abuse, emotional abuse, physical or emotional neglect, intimate partner violence, seeing mother treated violently by partner, household mental illness, parental separation or divorce, and incarceration of household member.

On a scale of 1-10, with 10 being highest, the higher the number of ACEs in an individual's history, the greater the likelihood of substance use disorders, behavioral problems, and an increase in chronic health problems.

In the general population, only about 25% of individuals have experienced four or more ACEs, and only 10% of the general population has experienced seven or more. However, in impoverished areas, that number is often far higher. Extreme poverty in rural communities is also an indicator of higher-than-normal ACE scores.

In our programs, that 10% quickly becomes 100% of our clients!

In our non-residential program at Foundation House, 100% of our clients have an ACE score of 4 or higher. Of those who need residential care, 100% have an ACE score of at least 7 and about 20% have a score of 10.

In contrast, most staff and volunteers in the majority of our church and nonprofit organizations have scores of 0-3.

I personally had a score of zero prior to my first marriage. Then it jumped up to seven. And then we divorced...

When children with high ACE scores grow up, they are more likely to act out their trauma in dangerous lifestyles such as addiction, criminal activity, incarceration, and gang violence. They are more likely to be either abusers or victims of abuse, as well.

The Prefrontal Cortex

Your brain develops from back to front, beginning with the brain stem in the womb and early infancy, and building slowly, through the years, toward your prefrontal cortex, which lies just behind your forehead.

The prefrontal cortex, in a typically developing person, begins to develop in adolescence and is fully developed by about age 24. Again, in a typically developing body. That's important.

The prefrontal cortex is where your brain accesses logic and forethought. It's where your brain understands the consequences of actions, and develops the skills for planning, prioritizing, and making good decisions.

However, as you can probably guess, the majority of our clients, regardless of their physical age, have not had the luxury of a "typically developing" brain. Because of the traumatic experiences, drug usage, and violence, many of our clients' brains were too focused on survival (remember Hot System dominance you just read above) to allow for a fully developed prefrontal cortex.

Between the underdevelopment of the prefrontal cortex and the damage from the overabundance of those survival chemicals, most of our clients think and act as if they are effectively 15 years old, regardless of their chronological age. Her brain development, his decision-making and reasoning skills, are all that of an adolescent—even in a 35-year-old's body.

Why It Matters

Trauma affects every aspect of them—body, soul, and spirit. In order for you to effectively serve, to love well, you must first understand that their brains work differently than yours does. You cannot expect her to think and reason like you. Trying to hold him to that level will only frustrate you, alienate him, and ultimately destroy any attempt you may have had to love them into a place of sustainable stability.

The trauma lens is absolutely *not* a "get out of jail free" card. It does, however, help you see more clearly the root issues which have led them to the situation that they now find themselves in. Through understanding how trauma affects brain development, you can more easily offer grace, compassion, and direction.

And *because* you can more easily offer grace and compassion and wisdom, you will quickly start to see the clients responding to you differently, receiving what you have to say in a fresh way. The more they can trust you not to judge them, not to make them feel badly for their life decisions, the faster they will begin to receive the course correction you offer.

When you work with clients, through a trauma lens, they will recognize it. They will receive you differently. They will listen more (although never 100%), and you'll begin seeing more consistent, more frequent client success than you thought possible. You'll start to see the client transformations that you knew were possible. And you will see these holistic life transformations too.

All because they know that you understand them, and they can trust in your love, secure in your support.

Lens Three – Addiction

Too many ministries are afraid of this population and so they issue a blanket refusal for anyone with an addiction history. But then they wonder why they have no clients…

Drug use, abuse, and addiction have skyrocketed across the US in the last decade, and especially since the 2020 pandemic. Partly because of the increase of cocaine, heroin, and fentanyl across our porous southern border and partly because meth is ridiculously easy to manufacture, the United States is suffering under an unprecedented level of addiction and drug-related deaths.

I could write *several* books on this topic alone, but others already have, so I'm only going to focus on the pieces which affect our typical clients.

1. Why

Our clients didn't start out using drugs with the intention of becoming homeless addicts, prostituting or stealing to maintain their habits. Virtually all of the women we serve at Foundation House originally discovered that the drug-induced high silenced their painful memories, at least for a little while. Their drug usage quickly became their *solution* to the actual problem: their trauma.

But drugs are rarely as potent as that first high, so dosage has to be continually increased. And it's in that chasing after the same high which leads to chemical dependency and addiction. And then, drug usage stops being about preventing the pain of their memories and serves to prevent the physical pain of detox (the "DTs").

Detoxing from certain drugs, like opiates, can trigger seizures, heart attacks, and death. It is imperative that you know what your clients have been taking so you can get them into appropriate medical detox programs.

2. But Why

Johann Hari says, "The opposite of addiction is not sobriety; it's connection." As these men and women begin using drugs, they become connected more deeply into drug culture, seeing themselves as society's outcasts and building a sense of pride, a self-identity, around that truth. Families of origin were either perpetrators of their abuse or were not helpful toward healing, plus many families cut ties with drug abusers over their actions. In this void, new relationships develop—whether as a street gang or a tight group of friends, becoming a new family unit.

In these relationships, our clients find acceptance and validation. And they also find peer pressure, which strengthens their reliance on these relationships while deepening their drug usage into abuse and then addiction. It's often in these relationships where our girls are introduced to heavier drugs, abusive dating relationships, and early criminal activity. A little theft, a little destruction of property. All in (their) fun.

Later, these criminal behaviors become necessary for survival as they deepen into addiction. They now need the drugs physically in order to survive, to prevent "the DT's," an incredibly painful detoxing from opioids. But still, it's the relationships which continue to propel these women forward. They may be trading sex for drugs but at least they have a safe place to sleep, and they also have the connection they crave.

And this is one reason why she fights against you or refuses to enter your program because she can't give up her phone. It's her connection to her friends who have become her (very dysfunctional) family. It's her lifeline. Which is also why it's so important for you to have at least a few weeks with her, without her phone, to build your own relationship before the birds of her past start stealing the seeds you're planting.

Some people can function for years at this level of drug abuse, a "functioning addict", but eventually, actions always have consequences. Physically, the drugs begin to take a toll on their face and bodies, especially teeth. Mentally, drugs begin affecting brain function, especially meth. At some point, the judicial system gets involved and stints in jail become a norm.

Friends begin to disappear, from overdose or prison, and fresh grief adds more layers of trauma which need to be silenced. And their drug abuse deepens.

3. <u>Ok but Why</u>

One thing we've learned over the years is that there are varying levels of addiction. There's physical addiction, which we've already discussed. There's also mental, emotional, and relational addiction.

One evidence of this is someone who has been in jail for six or eight months. Most people, including herself, assume that she is clean, no longer an addict. But that's usually not the case.

As a general rule, once she is out of jail, she almost always returns to her friend group, which leads back to drug usage and addiction—at the same or higher levels of drug usage as previously. This is one reason why overdose fatalities are so common, right out of jail. She has been physically clean for the last few months and so her body cannot handle the same level of drugs as it previously could. However, her brain clearly is still emotionally connected to the drugs. She still thinks like an addict. She still craves the drugs, and she remembers the high at the previous dosage levels.

And so that's where she resumes her drug usage, immediately.

Remember the story I shared in Chapter 4: after spending seven months in jail and then an additional five months with us while she completed her pregnancy, worked, and saved money to buy a car, the first thing Jamie did with her freedom was drive to her preferred trap house where she shot up with fentanyl. With her infant daughter in the car seat, along for the ride.

Jamie was physically no longer addicted but emotionally, mentally, she was absolutely still addicted.

Which is why we've added in a couple of layers of support, after physical detox, which are Relapse Prevention and Recovery Maintenance.

Relapse Prevention is mostly us still maintaining that protective bubble around her, being the structure that keeps her sober. Like a rehab program or jail, we provide physical barriers to her ability to fall back into active drug abuse. Sometimes, it's the pregnancy itself that motivates her to stay clean.

But eventually she has to leave the bubble, or her baby is born, and those external barriers have to move. Now comes the time where she will either relapse or she will maintain her own barriers. This is Recovery Maintenance, where she is taking ownership of her own sobriety. We provide encouragement and guidance as she learns to navigate a new life, learning to live with a new self-identity that is NOT an addict, worthless, homeless, trash, or whatever words that she's repeated to herself over the years.

Rescue Rebuild Restore

Lisa, our Director of Client Services, developed a Bible study for those who are ready to go deeper in learning how to live this new life. It's called Life After Grace and is built on Galatians 5:1 (AMP), "It was for this freedom that Christ set us free [completely liberating us]; therefore, keep standing firm and do not be subject again to a yoke of slavery [which you once removed].

You can learn more about bringing Life After Grace to your ministry, in the Resources section at the end of this book.

Once you've accepted God's grace, His salvation and forgiveness, how do you actually move forward building a new life, without constantly feeling the old guilt and shame, without constantly reminding yourself of what you did, what a terrible person you were? This Bible study is designed to teach clients how to live out that "life more abundant" that Jesus offers. God doesn't see us that way and we must learn to see ourselves differently too.

In offering her a new life, a new future, we have to remember that she needs the tools to *maintain* that new life. It's not good enough for her to merely experience life, grace, and hope briefly, while in our programs. If she cannot maintain it for herself and her children, we haven't benefited them whatsoever.

The reality is that drugs are unbelievably easy for her to find. She knows where to go, who to find, in order to score. We've had girls tell us stories of other employees (including the manager on duty) who were out back, getting high on their break time. Another client passed food through the drive-thru window to her former drug dealer. These girls can find drugs easily.

The trick is getting them to the point where they don't desire that life any longer. And then, getting them to the point where they don't even remember "the old days" of addiction, where the escape of a drug-induced haze is no longer their first urge after a long, stressful day.

When I'm speaking, I often equate drug addiction to sugar—or carb-addiction. It's an easy comparison, one many of us have dealt with, over the years. Obviously, no analogy is perfect. There are far fewer social problems associated with sugar addiction, and yet... I have lost weight many times throughout my adult life, only to gain it right back as soon as I loosened the strict rules I had lived under. I did a keto lifestyle and it worked great, until family birthdays and holidays created opportunities for one too many cheat days and, before I knew it, I was as addicted as I'd ever been.

There is a massive difference between physical addiction, which is easy to break with willpower and time, and emotional addiction, which requires a retraining of the brain, plus willpower and far more time than physical addiction typically requires.

The cravings are multi-layered. They are powerful. And they often carry fairly positive memories. When she's craving her old drug, she's remembering the pleasure of the high, not the horrors of her jail time, the loss of custody of her children, or the pain of her physical detoxing.

Just like when I'm craving something sweet, I'm recalling the memories of birthday cakes and Christmas cookies shared with loved ones. I'm remembering how pleasant the sweets taste and how it can take my mind off of my bills or my frustration, for a few minutes. I am absolutely not thinking about how quickly the scale jumps up, and how concerned the doctor is about my blood pressure.

Same principle. In order for recovery to become permanent, it starts with physical changes, yes, but that's only the beginning. Lasting recovery requires a permanent mind shift that no longer looks back to that former addiction fondly, that no longer craves, even in private, the pleasures of that old habit. And that takes a very long time.

Habits are incredibly difficult to break.

Viewing your client through this lens helps you understand how she could slide right back into her addiction, and even her concerns for her baby may not be enough to keep her sober. Your gentle yet firm protection is often the only thing holding her back from living out her worst fears—addiction, jail, and her baby in state custody. The grace you can offer isn't one of allowing her to regress to old habits and patterns but rather grace to understand how hard it is to hold onto her sobriety, often by her fingernails, and grace to wait until she feels a bit more stable before you push her toward the next goal on her case management list.

Lens Four – Mental Health

This lens is the most complicated of the four, because there are so many nuances, diagnoses, medications, and varying degrees of acceptance within society.

This category includes everything from depression and social anxiety to schizophrenia and Borderline Personality Disorder (BPD).

There's both a stigma and a status in a diagnosis. Sometimes the diagnosis gives them added state benefits, street cred, an explanation, or even an excuse. We've dealt with clients who were suicidal, clients who were paranoid-schizophrenic, and clients who were so angry (over past situations and people) that they could not self-regulate any *new* issues because their brains were so *full*—for lack of a better term—of their old, unresolved anger.

So, what do you do when you have no idea what to do? No idea what you're actually dealing with?

Figuring Them Out

First things first, we want to know exactly what is going on with our client. What is her current situation? Some clients will arrive on multiple medications (because it's all "free" through most state and federal Medicaid programs). Others will have prescriptions but refuse to take them. "I don't like how I feel" or "I don't want to put poison in my body"... when they are literally poisoning their bodies with drugs...

Still other clients have never been tested and yet, you *know* there is a presenting problem. Sometimes you can just *tell* that there is some kind of underlying factor. And some of the clients who arrive on multiple medications are actually mis-diagnosed OR over-medicated.

It's a tricky subject to attempt to tackle within the confines of this small chapter. The most important thing is to find out the truth, as quickly as possible.

We refer all of our prospective clients for a mental health evaluation, by a licensed provider. Locally, we have two state-funded mental health programs, but there are also many hospitals and health departments across the country with a psychiatrist on staff. Check your local area for appropriate providers.

And also, always <u>always</u> **always** ensure that the client signs a waiver allowing you to receive a copy of her evaluation and authorization to communicate with her doctor. The effort it takes to get it done is wasted if you cannot find out what was actually diagnosed, and what medications were prescribed. If your client refuses, then, in our program, that would be a massive red flag and could be grounds to refuse her entry into our residential program. We consider it that big of a deal.

Certain diagnoses or certain prescribed medications (things like Seroquel, Ativan, or any form of opioid pain management, Suboxone, or methadone treatment, etc.) should be huge red flags and probably deal-breakers for clients wanting to come into any type of residential program, unless you have a fully-equipped, 24/7, trained staff.

Another likely deal-breaker is if the client receives a diagnosis and is prescribed a treatment plan or medication, but then refuses to follow the doctor's recommendations.

Know which programs and treatment facilities exist in your area. Our local hospital has an in-patient psych ward, which can sometimes be necessary for proper diagnosis and medication-adjustment. It functions similarly to a detox program (from 7-28 days typically) and can also include a 6- to 12-week Intensive Outpatient Program (IOP) afterwards.

Although frequently, the only way for a client to actually access this in-patient treatment is for them to state to the program staff that they are feeling suicidal... Blame it on ridiculous government regulations or the hoops that have to be jumped through for the program to apply grant dollars to a specific client's case, there are myriad reasons why you may have to learn how to prep your clients to hold the truth a little loosely, or risk them not being able to access the medical treatment they desperately need.

Mental health can be an incredibly subjective issue. Without adequate training, it can be dangerous to work with certain clients. But also, it doesn't require *tons* of education or an advanced degree. You just need to know the important things, find good experts to partner with, and build systems for everyone's safety. Know your limits and also educate yourself so you can expand those boundaries, in wisdom.

The Rescue, Rebuild, Restore Framework

Now, you can probably see why our favorite way to teach the Rescue, Rebuild, Restore Framework is in person, through a multi-day workshop. This allows for questions and individualization which is next to impossible through pre-recorded lectures—and *no one* wants to sit through four days of virtual sessions!

In the next chapter and throughout Part 3, I'll share ways to implement this approach in your ministry within the limits of this book. Learning about the changes in the client's brain is the first step. Now, we need to know what to *do* with that knowledge.

Feeling like you're ready to talk with me now? Schedule a call with me to discuss whether Rescue, Rebuild, Restore is right for your ministry.

Key Chapter Takeaways
Poverty
- Material poverty is what most people think of when they hear the term, but it goes beyond that.
- Poverty mindset often goes with material poverty, but even the wealthy can have a poverty mindset.

- It is a worldview that sees only the lack around them, not resources. Not opportunities.
- Chronic poverty is often seen at a family or community level. It can include areas of food deserts, medical deserts, employment deserts, educational deserts, etc., where the entire community lives in physical lack of access to resources and opportunities.

Trauma
- Trauma is multi-faceted and is separate and distinct from the traumatic event.
- The sympathetic nervous system (hot system, survival mode) is the emergency response to the brain's awareness of a traumatic event.
  - The parasympathetic nervous system (cool system, growth mode) is the system in which the brain was designed to function normally.
  - Chronic trauma affects brain and body development in many ways, even causing harm to the brain itself.

Addiction
- Drug usage was often the original solution to the real problem of the chronic pain of trauma.
- Drug usage escalates into addiction and then a host of negative consequences ensue.
- Addiction is physical, mental, emotional and also relational.
- Emotional connection to addiction is far more difficult to break than physical addiction.

Mental Health
- It's a touchy subject and you definitely want to partner with local, like-minded professionals.

- But it's not impossibly scary. You don't need years of university training either.
- Make sure you have access to all of her medical records. You need a complete picture to fully understand whether you are equipped to take her on.

Chapter 7: Rescue

So what do we do with all the information we've just learned? How do we translate our new understanding of poverty, trauma, and addiction into practical solutions for the people we serve?

As followers of Christ, we are called to love the least of these with compassion, wisdom, and action—rescuing them from the overwhelming challenges of poverty, trauma, addiction, and mental health. In the RRR framework, the *Rescue* phase is the critical first step, rooted in unconditional love and understanding the brain and body differences shaped by their experiences. This chapter explores how to translate our new insights into practical, individualized solutions, using the Rescue, Rebuild, Restore Framework to serve wisely and effectively.

As you read these pages, reflect on the people you're currently serving, those you've worked with in the past, and those you've seen others help. Look for similarities to what I share, but also for differences and nuances—areas where you may not fully agree. We humans are unique, and our lived experiences are uniquely shaped by God's design. While I'll share stories that fit this model, others may not, reminding us to hold everything loosely, avoiding rigid molds that never work.

A Prophetic Vision for Rescue

Several years ago, I received a profound dream I believe was a prophetic gift from the Lord, shaping my understanding of our call as the Church to serve the poor and disenfranchised.

Picture an ocean near cliffs, with icy, choppy, dangerous waters. My boat, anchored and stable yet riding the waves, stands ready. A ship has capsized, and many people—fearful, panicked, confused, or dazed—float past in the water. I reach down, lifting them into the boat.

As the ones who have been rescued are now cared for, with towels, medical attention, food and rest, some begin to turn and join me at the sides of the boat, rescuing yet more. Miraculously, the boat never overflows; there's always room for more, expanding as the rescued become rescuers, pulling yet others from the icy depths.

It is within this dream that Foundation House developed our tagline: <u>Rescuing Mothers, Rebuilding Lives, Restoring Futures</u> and I discovered my personal assignment: to rescue an entire generation of mothers, equipping them to rescue their own children, and celebrating when some of their children will not need rescuing in the first place.

Our task is collective:
- Set anchor in the right place, directed by God.
- Stabilize ourselves in the boat, secure in Christ.
- Pull others out and stabilize them.
- Train them to rescue more, creating a ripple of transformation.

Rescue Rebuild Restore

With this picture in mind, let's explore the step-by-step process of *Rescue*, *Rebuild*, and *Restore*, beginning with *Rescue*.

Step 1: Rescue

Chances are, this is the piece that you're already doing... Or at least you think you're already doing

Are you a Rescuer or are you a Sustainer?

You're likely already engaged in some form of help—perhaps food pantries, homeless shelters, or emergency aid. But are you rescuing, or merely sustaining? By definition, rescuing pulls someone entirely out of their situation, like lifting a person from the ocean into a boat and taking them to shore.

Sustaining, like tossing a life preserver, helps them survive longer but doesn't remove them from danger—they're still drowning.

Most ministries to the poor and disenfranchised are sustainers, not rescuers. Food pantries and shelters provide vital life support, but they often fail to make a long-term impact, leaving people in cycles of poverty, trauma, or addiction. This isn't a judgment—sustaining ministries serve a crucial purpose—but we must recognize the difference.

Why choose sustaining over rescuing? Time and money are key factors; rescuing demands far more of both. But we must also consider the receiver's readiness. Unlike the panicked souls in my dream, many we serve have acclimated to their current state—content in survival mode, shaped by poverty mindsets, chronic trauma, or addiction.

Change is hard, and rescue carries expectations: an addict entering a 30-day treatment program is expected to stay clean, but what if they're not ready, don't want to stop, or fear the consequences of change? Sustaining programs will always be needed, as many aren't prepared for lasting transformation.

<u>Please do not hear this as a value judgment against sustainer ministries.</u> They are incredibly vital and they serve a great purpose. However, you need to understand there is a definite difference between rescuing and sustaining.

Those probably seemed like some big value judgements. You may be kinda mad at me right now. That's okay. Shoot me an email. Let's talk about it. Suzanne@becharitywise.com

Rescuing Wisely

Rescuing feels heroic—pulling a young woman from domestic violence, a single mom into your home, or a homeless man into employment. It's the stuff of movies, but the reality is less glamorous—dirty, scary, and intimidating, yet deeply rewarding.

I've sat with someone who was high, falling asleep mid-intake; rushed to help a woman gather documents before her abusive partner returned; faced threats from angry exes demanding she leave our program. These moments are a rush—holding someone's life and future in your hands—but they require wisdom, not just excitement.

There are three primary tasks of the Rescue phase.

1. <u>Stabilization</u> is crucial for ensuring that your client can begin to move toward trusting you, allowing themselves to be rescued. Like grasping a flailing person's forearm while they're still in the water, stabilization might mean detox programs, motel rooms, or sustaining aid like food and shelter. The difference is your commitment to the long haul,

understanding their poverty, trauma, or addiction as temporary states, not permanent identities.

2. <u>Trust-building</u> is relationship-building, proving you're trustworthy—doing what you say, like picking them up on time or following through on promises. Receivers, shaped by manipulation and conditional love (as discussed in Chapter 4), have little reason to trust. They need time to risk believing you won't repeat past hurts, especially given their trauma or addiction histories. They have no reason to trust you. You must consistently, repeatedly, prove yourself *trustworthy*.

3. And, during this entire early process, you're <u>Gathering Data.</u> Learn about your client—their likes, dislikes, history, habits—to demonstrate care and concern. At Foundation House, we use tools like Love Languages tests to show love in ways they feel most deeply, like bringing their favorite drink or recognizing triggers for old temptations. Know them, see them, love them, tailoring your approach to their unique poverty, trauma, addiction, or mental health needs.

Know them. See them. Love them.

<u>Potential Fatal Flaws in Rescuing Wisely</u>

Rescuing carries weighty responsibilities, with three pitfalls to avoid:

1. <u>Eternal Salvation</u>: Some ministries require worship attendance or a "sinner's prayer" for help, creating a "pay-to-play" environment where receivers might fake faith to access aid. I'm concerned about "goats in sheep's clothing"—people believing they're saved but hearing Jesus say, "Depart from Me, I never knew you" (Matthew 7:23). We point to Jesus, but forcing salvation risks undermining genuine heart change. As 1 Corinthians 13:3 warns, acts without love gain nothing.

2. <u>Control</u>: Rescuers often wield power, directing decisions—like telling clients where to go or what to do, as we do initially at Foundation House. This can keep receivers in a passive, victim mindset, trapped in a "helpless" box. Like crabs pulling each other back into a bucket, we may unintentionally hinder their growth, assuming they can't make choices or maintain stability (e.g., denying mental health meds, setting unattainable expectations).

3. <u>No Good Deed Goes Unpunished</u>: Kindhearted actions can backfire due to "compassionate arrogance"—ignorance-driven confidence that we can handle any situation, even unwise ones. Shepherding homes, like foster care, require trauma training, background checks, and support, but jumping in without preparation risks harm. I've seen volunteers move clients into homes, only to face resentment, relapse, or heartbreak, reinforcing receivers' shame or bitterness.

Behaviors to Expect in Rescue Mode

Receivers in rescue mode, shaped by poverty, trauma, addiction, or mental health, often exhibit:

- Resistance or Manipulation: Survival tactics, like manipulation, stem from trauma's sympathetic nervous system activation or poverty mindsets, expecting rejection or control.
- Relapse or Regression: Addicts may return to drugs, domestic violence survivors to abusers (with 70% recidivism rates post-jail or relapse rates for addiction), or homeless individuals to instability, due to emotional ties or unmet needs.
- Distrust or Fear: Conditioned by conditional love, they may fear trust, testing boundaries or withdrawing, especially with mental health challenges.

- Passivity or Helplessness: Learned helplessness or entitlement mentalities may keep them reliant, unable to take initiative without guidance.

Responses That Encourage Growth

To move receivers toward *Rebuild* and *Restore*, respond with:
- Patience and Grace: Allow time for stabilization and trust, recognizing their brain and body differences from trauma or addiction, as Chapter 7 notes.
- Empowerment, Not Control: Gradually relinquish control, offering choices (e.g., Love Languages, goal-setting) to build self-efficacy, countering helplessness.
- Trauma-Informed Care: Understand their poverty mindsets, addiction triggers, or mental health needs, creating flexible, safe rules that foster growth, not shame.
- Unconditional Love: Love as Christ does, believing in their potential, even in relapse or resistance, as 1 Corinthians 13:7 declares, "Love never takes failure as defeat, for it never gives up."
- Partnership with Professionals: Collaborate with experts for addiction, trauma, or mental health, ensuring wise, individualized support.

Moving Forward in Faith

Rescuing isn't glamorous but vital, requiring us to anchor in God's love, stabilize ourselves, and pull others out with wisdom. Some will stay in rescue mode permanently, others will grow into rescuers, but all need our patience and grace. In the chapters ahead, we'll explore *Rebuild* and *Restore*, building on this foundation. For now, let us pray for the courage to rescue wisely, trusting God to transform lives, one unique heart at a time.

Self-Assessment: Evaluating Your Rescue Approach

Use this assessment to reflect on your approach to rescuing. Rate each statement on a scale of 1-5 (1 = Strongly Disagree, 5 = Strongly Agree). Total your score to gauge your readiness and identify areas for growth.

- I focus on rescuing receivers—pulling them out of poverty, trauma, or addiction—rather than just sustaining them with temporary aid.

- I prioritize building trust with receivers, understanding their fear or resistance due to past manipulation or trauma.

- I gather data about receivers' unique needs (e.g., likes, history, triggers) to tailor my approach, showing love in ways they feel most deeply.

- I avoid imposing control, empowering receivers to make choices and grow, even if it feels uncomfortable or risky.

- I trust God to transform receivers' lives, even when they resist, relapse, or exhibit learned helplessness or entitlement.

- I recognize the cost of rescuing—time, effort, and heartbreak—and am willing to pay it, as Christ calls us to love unconditionally.

- I partner with professionals or seek training to handle complex issues like addiction, trauma, or mental health wisely, not acting alone.

- I ensure my ministry doesn't create a "pay-to-play" environment, pointing receivers to Jesus without forcing salvation.

- I remain patient and gracious, even when receivers test boundaries or regress, believing in their potential for growth.

Rescue Rebuild Restore

Scoring:

- 9-18: You may need to deepen your rescue approach, seeking God's guidance to serve with wisdom and patience.

- 19-36: You're making progress, but there's room to refine your methods, focusing on trust and empowerment.

- 37-45: Your rescue approach is strong and faith-filled, but continue seeking His wisdom to sustain your ministry.

Chapter 8: Rebuild

For a person to stay rescued, the things, people, thoughts, behaviors they were once accustomed to, now all need to be replaced with *other* things, people, thoughts, and beliefs. The discomfort of this transition, from known yet unhelpful to new and untested, can lead to a sense of codependency between the rescued and the rescuer. And there's nothing wrong with that, to a *very* limited point.

Think of a child, just learning how to walk. They need to hold onto something or someone else to maintain their stability. But that doesn't last very long and soon, they are running around independently.

What works in toddlers also works in adults. Dependency of the *rescued* on the *rescuer* is a necessary step in the process. Where it becomes unhealthy is when it persists, when the rescuer feeds that dependency and creates a codependent relationship which is unhealthy for both the rescued and the rescuer.

Side note:__ Please don't hear me as if I'm saying that the rescued are toddlers. Nooo. Of course not. These are patterns of learning and behavior that are universal to humans and so sometimes it's easier to view the pattern in children or in animals or in something else that is separate and distinct from the person standing in front of you. This allows you to distinguish the pattern from the person, enabling you to understand what is happening under their surface without making judgments (which could be unfair or unfounded) toward the individual. Same reason Jesus taught in parables: Look at what is happening in this story or see it in this alternate situation, and then apply that, in wisdom, to what you're dealing with right now.

Many times, rescuers enjoy the feeling of pride in having helped someone. They may enjoy being looked up to by the rescued person. They may feel a paternal sense of protection and responsibility toward the person they've rescued. This may be one of the few people in the rescuer's life who appreciates them, who is grateful for them. It can be a heady feeling to know that you are the reason another person is alive and safe. Heady but inappropriate.

Building Self-Efficacy Through Trust

In the Rebuild phase, the goal is to help others <u>only as much</u> as they actually need your help, and to encourage and equip them to begin to do more and more for themselves. This is why that savior complex, that unhealthy level of continued dependency, is so harmful.

Self-efficacy, according to the American Psychological Association, refers to "an individual's belief in his or her capacity to execute behaviors necessary to produce specific performance attainments. Self-efficacy reflects confidence in the ability to exert control over one's own motivation, behavior and social environment."

Self-efficacy is an internal understanding of one's own ability to do or to think. We might call it self-confidence or self-assurance, but it is rooted in <u>evidence</u>. We humans generally need proof that we can accomplish something before we will even attempt it.

Self-efficacy can be developed in several ways:

1. Mastery experiences: Giving others opportunities to attempt and either succeed or learn through failure—the strongest source of growth.
2. Emotional and physiological states: Recognizing when they're ready or "in the mood" for change, respecting their pace.
3. Encouragement and social persuasion: Offering positive peer support, not pressure, to build confidence.
4. Vicarious experiences: Learning through role models, mentors, or stories of overcoming.

Self-efficacy and growth mindset are what we call "domain-specific" in the brain science world. This means that we can have self-efficacy and a growth mindset in *one* area of our lives but still maintain a fixed mindset in another area. For example, I have a growth mindset in many areas but, when it comes to math, I tend to have a fixed mindset. (I often joke that I went into social services to *avoid* math!)

What damages self-efficacy? Discouragement.

In fact, discouragement is better at *reducing* self-efficacy in a person than encouragement is at *increasing* it. So many of the people we serve have been living in a perpetual state of discouragement for years, maybe decades. It's no wonder that so few believe they can accomplish something. They've been discouraged out of believing in themselves.

The whole point of this Rebuild phase is to both teach and also give opportunities for them to see themselves as capable of learning and doing. Building self-efficacy through evidence, through experience, equips people with *proof* that they can do it.

Ways to Build Self-Efficacy

1. Practice
2. Try new things
3. Find role models (stories of overcomes, mentors, friendships)
4. Build a support system (continued relationships)
5. Be positive. Think positive.
6. Reflect on past actions, remember successes and lessons learned.

Let's revisit that analogy of a toddler learning how to walk. First, they crawl, cheered on by parents and caregivers. Then, they begin pulling themselves up on furniture, or a parent holds their hands while they stand and begin practicing steps. They then take a few toddling steps, independently though, they fall down frequently. And before long, they are racing around the house, as if they've always known how.

Building self-efficacy in teens and adults works in the exact same process. First, they need a lot of support and encouragement, correction and modeling. Then, they need freedom to experiment, to try it out for themselves, in a safe environment where they have no fears of censure or rejection. And then, finally, they need the self-authority, the autonomy, to freely do things their own way. This applies whether they are learning to read, to work a job, or raise their children.

Rescue Rebuild Restore

The process from lack of knowledge to competency and self-efficacy is exactly the same, regardless of age, gender, or area of growth.

Fatal Flaws in Rebuilding

There are two ways in which all of this can go horribly, horribly wrong. One way is rooted in the person you're helping, but the other belongs entirely to you. Before you get mad and throw this book (or your ereader) across the room, let's talk about *them* first…

1. When in Doubt, Blow It Up

Before we can move to the Restore phase, we need to talk about a powerful detour that many, many of our clients will take instead—self-sabotage.

For a large majority of your clients, you will find that the higher they rise in stability, the more uncomfortable and unstable they feel.

There's a wonderful scene at the end of the old movie, *White Christmas,* where Bing Crosby's character tells Rosemary Clooney's character that being the knight in shining armor, high up on that tall horse, is intimidating and lonely. What if he fails? What if he falls? That's a super-short paraphrase.

Nevertheless, the principle is the same. Imagine that you're standing on the floor in your office. You need to go higher so you climb onto your desk. That's a pretty stable piece of furniture (I assume), but if you fall, it could hurt. Now, your assignment is to go even higher. So, you grab a chair to set on top of your desk. Way less stable and also, if you fall from this new height, it will hurt a whole lot more.

Now, let's shift that principle back to the people we are called to serve.

How about we use Brooke as an example? Remember her story from Chapter 1? Brooke has lived with us for the majority of the last four and a half years (leaving once for several months after the birth of her first child, returning again in a worse condition than she had been when she first arrived). She has a long history of trauma and abuse, some perpetrated by her parents, some by others. And, eventually, she became the catalyst for her own abuse as she prostituted for money and drugs. She has had an extensive history of meth addiction and also several mental health diagnoses, for which she is finally correctly medicated, and cognitive delays which will hinder her from ever living fully independently.

She recently celebrated three years clean and graduated from our residential program. However, for Brooke, graduation does not look like it usually does for other clients. She cannot live independently yet she is too advanced for the local residential programs for those with developmental disabilities. She has no family to return to; both of her parents are deceased. And so, Brooke has consistently self-sabotaged at every previous attempt (of ours) to graduate.

The difference this time? We ignored her. Well, not her specifically. We ignored her behaviors, comments, and attitudes because we knew where they were rooted: In fear of the unknown. Fear of what will come next for her. Perhaps even some grief that her future doesn't quite look like the futures of some of the other girls she has watched graduate and move out of our program, building their own independent lives.

So, you may be asking, why make Brooke graduate at all? Especially if we plan to keep her with us 'til Jesus returns?

It's a good question but also a short-sighted one. Brooke needed to graduate. She has completed all of our courses at least twice, and some we created just for her. She is the shift leader in our main job-training program (a thrift shop). She has also been asking about graduation. When would she graduate? What would that look like? Would we say nice things about her on stage, in front of a room full of nicely dressed people?

Brooke needed to graduate to demonstrate to herself that she could complete a program. We are not the first program Brooke has attempted, but we *are* the place where she has found success, stability, and a home. She needed to graduate to codify that growth and success in her own heart and mind.

And yet, she also asked a bazillion questions for months leading up to her graduation at our winter fundraising event. Fear and anticipation battled within her. What *would* her life look like after graduation? She had emotional meltdowns. She rebelled against rules and responsibilities that she never balked at before—everything from cleaning her room to picking up an extra shift in the thrift shop to adequately maintaining her personal hygiene.

Self-sabotage.

The very things she feared the most, disappointment, being let down or abandoned, failing yet again, she attempted to trigger in the months leading up to graduation. But we were prepared. When she tried to pick a fight, we called her out. We reminded her how much we loved her and reassured her once again that we may not like her behavior too much right now, but we still love her and that will never change.

Brooke needs to know that she can never be bad enough for us to stop loving her. Although there are things she could do which would require her to leave our home, we would still love her. She has left and returned once before, and she knows how near death (literally, that is not hyperbole) she was when she returned to us. She often thanks us for letting her come back and saving her life.

She knows the truth and yet, she is now in a place where she has never been before. Who is she if she's not an addict and a failure? Who is she if she's not hustling for men or money? Who is this new Brooke? It is scary to step forward into an unknown future. Standing taller than she has ever stood before.

Falling from the height of meth-addicted prostitute isn't that far... Falling from successful program graduate, clean for three years, shift leader and mentor to new clients in the program? That is a much scarier height from which to fall. A much more painful landing.

Self-sabotage is nothing more than preemptively acting on fear, creating a self-fulfilling prophecy in the process.

Another example for you: Many times, over the years, clients have come in with a personal history of being in foster care. Typically, those were not pleasant memories and the client has a lot of fear around her child also ending up in state custody. Yet, here she is, entering our program because she is homeless, a recent addict (we don't accept anyone in active addiction—they must detox first before coming into our home), and in danger of the exact scenario she most fears.

Yet, rather than listening to us and embracing this opportunity for full life transformation, she is bitter, rebellious, defiant, stubborn. She has been caring for herself for years, so she knows far better than all of us, who live in houses and own cars and are married to men who don't beat us.

Inevitably, there are a small handful who act rashly enough that we have to be the ones to contact our local Child Abuse hotline and trigger an investigation into her ability to care for her child.

Fear. Fear is what triggers all of it. Brooke's fears had her attempting every way she could to self-destruct. We refused to allow it to happen.

Fear tricks these mamas into believing lies and half-truths and blowing up their lives, causing far more destruction than anyone from the outside ever could. Fear has moms returning to abusive men, and marrying them. Fear has moms returning to drugs because they cannot handle the hard work of dealing with their trauma, healing and creating something new.

Fear.

Take a look at Kelley & Connor's Emotional Cycle of Change study.

Kelley and Conner's Emotional Cycle of Change

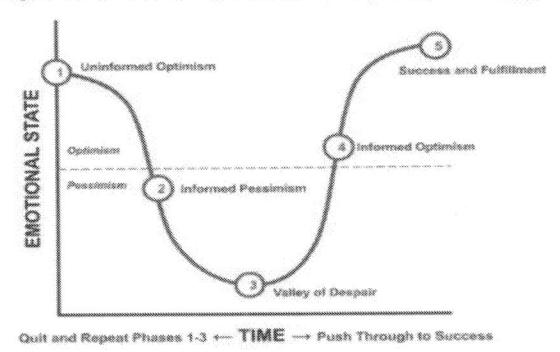

EMOTIONAL STATE

1. Uninformed Optimism
2. Informed Pessimism
3. Valley of Despair
4. Informed Optimism
5. Success and Fulfillment

Quit and Repeat Phases 1-3 ←— TIME —→ Push Through to Success

The reason we are able to so blithely allow Brooke to annoy everyone with her attempts at self-sabotage is what we learned from this chart right here. All we are doing is refusing to allow her to push us all out of the Valley of Despair and back to Uninformed Optimism. The only way we will ever escape the Valley is to power through it.

Some challenges can be avoided. Some can be short-cut. But some have to be tackled head on.

This graph demonstrates how people grow through change. We all start out wide-eyed, excited, and ignorant and then reality comes crashing in.

New volunteers invariably best demonstrate this process. Everyone always wants to work with our girls, love on them, rock our sweet babies... until they discover the girls *aren't* grateful. The babies, though sweet, also often have issues after birth which cause them to cry and fuss more frequently. They aren't always cuddly. Sometimes they have medical conditions which cause pain and discomfort and need certain interventions, which unfortunately take us a while to understand.

Surely it's supposed to be easier than this, many wonder. Did God actually call me here? Maybe I'll go volunteer at the animal shelter or get a part time job at Target, instead.

Unfortunately, they're just chasing that shiny object back to the realm of Uninformed Optimism. What people don't understand is that the only way to get to where they want to go, Success and Fulfillment, is to traverse the journey *through* the Valley of Despair. This part of the journey cannot be avoided, cannot be short-cut. It must be traveled. Lessons must be learned, sacrifices made, false beliefs and misplaced expectations must be laid at the feet of Jesus as we follow Him to the heart of the Father. This is part of counting the cost that we discussed in Chapter 4.

Since discovering this research from Kelley and Connor, we have begun sharing it over and over—with clients, volunteers, staff, and other ministries alike. It has given language to behaviors we've observed over and over, which has allowed us to better pinpoint when our clients, volunteers, staff, and donors are struggling with their desire to retreat back to Uninformed Optimism. Ignorance really is bliss.

2. Back Off, Dude

Okay, now it's your turn. How can *you* derail or destroy someone else's progress?

By pushing too hard, too fast.

For any change to become permanent, we humans need time for our minds and bodies to adapt to a new normal. Think about it in terms of weight loss—lots of people can lose weight. The real trick is *keeping* it off. There are two ways in which our bodies communicate that they need time to rest and reset as we lose weight—plateaus and maintenance mode. (Shoutout to my friend, Samantha, and her excellent book *The Calories and Confidence Method*, which helped me understand the importance of the maintenance phase insert link).

Plateaus and Recovery Saturation

In the weight-loss world, a plateau is generally depicted as a negative. When we have been losing weight and suddenly stop, that's called "hitting a plateau." Traditional advice says that our next assignment is to reduce our carb intake more dramatically, or increase our exercise levels. The goal is to add or remove something that will get us back to consistent weight loss, right?

But we've misunderstood the purpose of plateaus for years. It's not evidence that you're somehow failing, but rather that you're moving too fast for your body to keep up.

Think about a physical plateau, a flat area at a higher elevation. You're climbing a mountain and you come across a flat area. What are you going to do? Rest. Eat your lunch. Breathe and acclimate to the higher altitude with its thinner air. And when you're refreshed, you resume your climb to the summit. You now have the energy, the stamina, the fortitude to persevere.

It's <u>on the plateau</u> that your body has time to rest, reset, heal, before tackling the next level.

Your body needs time to allow itself to learn this new level, to create a "new normal." Whether we're talking about losing weight, climbing a mountain, or remembering to pack your baby's diaper bag the night before, your brain and your body function exactly the same.

Our Director of Operations, Lisa Holmes, has coined the term "recovery saturation" to depict the point at which our clients reach a certain level of new knowledge and experiences. Like a sponge, they need time to allow it all to absorb before they can attempt to receive anything further.

It's a fascinating perspective. One that I think many of us, if we take a moment, can understand as we consider our own lives. Have you ever attended a weeklong conference of some type? Whether a work conference or a week of revival meetings?

I, for one, often reach a point where my brain feels "full," as if I can't take in anything further. I need to process and allow it all to be absorbed. Then I'll be ready for the next new thing.

For whatever reason, we humans have a tendency to recognize this process in ourselves and yet, for others, we offer little in the way of grace. Maybe it's because we can feel when our brain is too full, but we can't see it in someone else. Maybe we are quick to presume that they are "lazy" or "rebelling" or some other negative accusation which increases our feeling of superiority and diminishes their own perspective.

Whatever the reason, it's damaging to the trust you've worked so hard to build in the Rescue phase.

Maintenance Mode

As I've mentioned, this concept was introduced to me by my good friend, health expert Samantha Bahr, author of *The Calories and Confidence Method*.

One of the concepts Sam teaches is that once we reach a goal (weight), our body requires roughly the same length of time to settle to this new weight as our body's baseline as it did to achieve this new level, to begin with. So, for example, if it took you 12 weeks to lose a set amount of weight, your body is still conditioned to the old weight as its "normal." It will take your body an additional 12 weeks for it to recognize "this" as its new baseline.

This is the root issue behind yo-yo diets, losing weight only for you to gain it all back once your diet is over. Your body never got the opportunity to reset itself to a new level, a new baseline.

Too often, we are pushing our clients from one goal to the next without giving them time in between to acclimate. She got a job and is now consistently showing up, for the first time ever. She's not using drugs to cope. A baby is coming and she's pretty freaked out—excited, scared, and unsure of either of their futures. Now we're pushing her to buy a car, finish her GED, pick a college to attend, and plan to move into an apartment of her own when she's never done any of these things before. It's too much too fast. And we, the rescuer, often don't recognize the burden we're adding to our clients. They want to please us, they trust us. But when we push too hard, they tend to freeze, to regress, or to run away.

She's responding exactly as she always has to overwhelm and fear. We are the ones who need to slow down and allow her brain and her body to adjust.

Faith and Failure(s)

And the biggest issue with all of this is that *you* hold their faith in a tenuous position. Your behavior and attitude toward them will affect their understanding of Jesus and the Kingdom of God. You get the privilege and responsibility to demonstrate either the love of Christ or reinforce that we Christians are just hypocrites and liars.

That's a weighty position to find yourself in. In Chapter 9, we're going to shift gears to the primary goal for all of our clients—full restoration.

Self-Assessment: Evaluating Your Rebuild Approach

Use this assessment to reflect on your approach to rebuilding. Rate each statement on a scale of 1-5 (1 = Strongly Disagree, 5 = Strongly Agree). Total your score to gauge your readiness and identify areas for growth.

- I focus on building receivers' self-efficacy, giving them opportunities to succeed or learn, rather than maintaining dependency.

- I recognize when receivers self-sabotage due to fear or discomfort, responding with patience and reassurance, not frustration.
- I avoid pushing receivers too hard or too fast, allowing time for their brains and bodies to acclimate to new stability.
- I provide role models, encouragement, and support systems to help receivers develop trust and confidence in their abilities.
- I trust God to guide receivers through the Emotional Cycle of Change, even when they struggle in the Valley of Despair.
- I check my own pride or savior complex, ensuring I empower receivers to take responsibility, not remain passive.
- I understand how poverty, trauma, addiction, or mental health shape receivers' resistance, tailoring my approach with grace.
- I celebrate small steps and past successes with receivers, building evidence of their potential for growth.
- I remain committed to rebuilding, even when receivers fail or relapse, trusting in God's transformative power.

Scoring:
- 9-18: You may need to deepen your Rebuild approach, seeking God's guidance to serve with patience and empowerment.
- 19-36: You're making progress, but there's room to refine your methods, focusing on self-efficacy and timing.
- 37-45: Your rebuild approach is strong and faith-filled, but continue seeking His wisdom to sustain your ministry.

Chapter 9: Restore

This phase is one that few of your clients will achieve while still working with you. It's also the place where you have the least control. If we equate the three phases to raising kids (yeah, I know I use this analogy a lot— I literally raise mamas and their kids every day 🪦 🧤), it would look kinda like this:

- Rescue: Like infants, toddlers, and elementary schoolers, receivers are incapable of managing on their own, needing love, support, and full care to stabilize amidst poverty, trauma, or addiction.
- Rebuild: Like adolescents, they grow more capable but need practice, experimentation, and encouragement to build self-efficacy, overcoming codependency and fixed mindsets.
- Restore: Like late teens to early adults, they must take ownership to learn permanence, while still welcoming suggestions and support, trusting God's timing over ours.

I often find that the givers who struggle the most with this phase are the ones who haven't raised their kids into adulthood yet. Parents of young children simply don't have the lived experience of gradually relinquishing authority to someone else. It's a difficult path to navigate, allowing someone else to control the reins of their own lives. That's not to say these parents can't learn, of course, but rather that they don't already have lived experience to draw from as they work with adults in challenging situations.

With this in mind, let's dive into the Restore process.

<u>Restore</u> really is very similar to empowering teenagers to take ownership of their own lives. As a parent of adult children, all married and two now with children of their own, I have experienced a wide array of emotions as these beautiful, sweet, snuggly little babies have grown up through the terrible twos, the rambunctious elementary years, the moody and rebellious teen years and now they are all happily content in early adulthood, gainfully employed, living in their own homes, raising children, and serving both God and their community. My husband and I are very proud of all three of our kids, their spouses, and their babies. Grandkids truly are the best gift.

When I first started Foundation House, our older son was in the 8th grade and our younger son was in 1st Grade. I learned how to parent teens alongside learning to navigate this ministry and the varied client personalities the Lord sent us. One of the most crucial things I learned during that season was to allow the Holy Spirit to do what He knows each person needs.

1. **Trusting Holy Spirit**

Trust Holy Spirit. This is probably the true heart of our individualized service to each client—the understanding that Holy Spirit knows far better than we staff how to guide each of these girls unto salvation, unto Father God, unto their best future.

In the Restore phase, common activities we see are: single moms beginning to date, buy cars, find freedom, use it poorly and then learn, often only in hindsight, what dumb decisions they can still make.

We've learned that Holy Spirit knows exactly when and how to bring correction that is useful, never arbitrary or punitive.

An example of potentially arbitrary responses, which could have become punitive, is in the love story of my youngest son, Ethan, and his sweet wife, Stevi.

They met in youth group, dated through high school, and married shortly after graduation. Our pastor, Dustin, once enforced a no-dating rule for youth, fearing hormones and emotions, but Ethan and Stevi's story showed how rigid rules can harm God's plan. Trusting the Holy Spirit means avoiding arbitrary actions, as Proverbs 3:5-6 urges: "Trust in the Lord with all your heart and lean not on your own understanding; in all your ways submit to Him, and He will make your paths straight." We must trust Him with our clients, children, and ourselves, knowing He is trustworthy.

2. **Accepting Free Will**

This section is all about coming to terms with the reality that each of your clients (like your children) have free will and can choose to do what they want, regardless of your opinions. Sometimes in direct opposition to our opinions!

Sometimes, in the exercising of their free will, our clients make decisions that we don't agree with. Whether that's leaving our programs too early, getting involved in unhealthy relationships, falling back into old patterns, or simply refusing to grow beyond a certain point, we have to accept that, not only do they have permission to decide their own lives, but also Holy Spirit knows exactly what and when and how they need to traverse their pathway in order for them to come to an understanding of God's holy sovereignty over their lives. (See #1 above.) We humans often only learn in hindsight.

I remember, years ago, when Foundation House was in its infancy, the then-director of our local domestic violence shelter spoke at an event about the high numbers of women who return to domestic violence situations. She said that sometimes a woman comes back to their shelter, yet again, with a broken nose or arm, and this may *seem* like failure, but it's actually great progress. She said, "The first relationship, she spent three years beaten and abused. This time, it took a mere three weeks for her to realize what was happening." That is a definition of success.

The progress is incremental sometimes, but it is progress nevertheless. Your challenge is not to see small, incremental

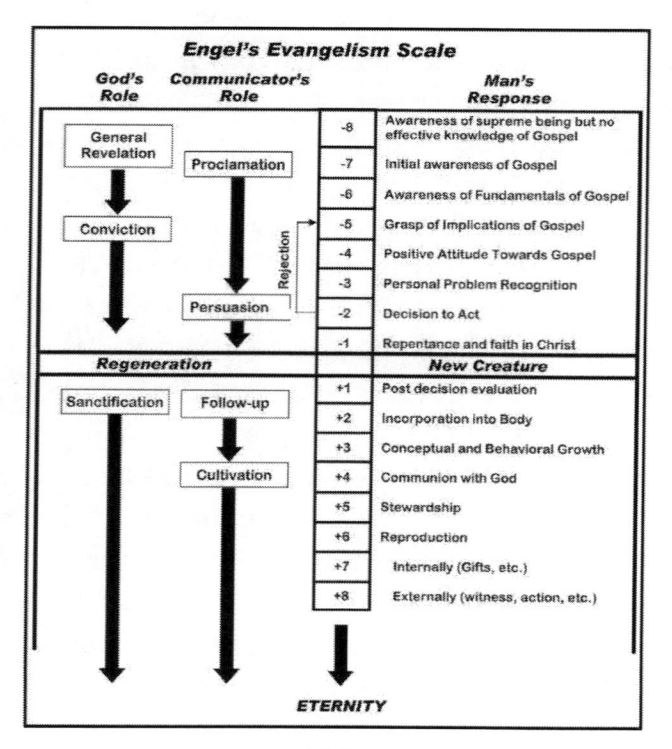

Engel's Evangelism Scale

God's Role	Communicator's Role		Man's Response
General Revelation		-8	Awareness of supreme being but no effective knowledge of Gospel
	Proclamation	-7	Initial awareness of Gospel
		-6	Awareness of Fundamentals of Gospel
Conviction		-5	Grasp of Implications of Gospel
		-4	Positive Attitude Towards Gospel
		-3	Personal Problem Recognition
	Persuasion	-2	Decision to Act
		-1	Repentance and faith in Christ
Regeneration			**New Creature**
Sanctification	Follow-up	+1	Post decision evaluation
		+2	Incorporation into Body
		+3	Conceptual and Behavioral Growth
	Cultivation	+4	Communion with God
		+5	Stewardship
		+6	Reproduction
		+7	Internally (Gifts, etc.)
		+8	Externally (witness, action, etc.)

ETERNITY

progress as failure but rather to accept it for what it is. Progress. Period.

Engel's Scale of Evangelism is a fantastic tool to understand change, transformation, and growth. It's also the only scale I've ever seen which honors the negative. Take a look at the following chart.

The negative numbers are before Salvation. Going from a 0 to 1 is that first step into saving knowledge of Jesus Christ, and then the positive numbers reflect increasing growth and maturity in our faith.

We all want to see these people saved, their names written in the Lamb's Book of Life and their daily lives looking similar to our own: regular church attendance, personal stability, and a compassionate heart to serve others.

However...

As with the Rebuild phase, we can't control what others *do* with the opportunities we offer them. Sometimes, we are called to lead a 0 into a +1, and we celebrate alongside the angels. Sometimes, however, our sole assignment from the Lord was to bring them from a -10 to a -8. That is still great progress, celebrated in the Kingdom of God.

Someone else may then have the assignment of bringing them to a -4, then -2 and eventually, guided step by step by Holy Spirit, they enter into the Kingdom of God through the efforts of yet another person or ministry. We all want to be the one to help these friends, these clients, these "least of these" whom Jesus loves, into salvation, and yet...

"I plant and Apollos waters, but it is God who causes the increase."

This is actually an incredibly freeing lesson for your volunteers and staff to understand. The two sections above work in tandem. When we allow Holy Spirit permission to be the Decider, the Director, of our steps, He gives us the grace and patience we need to accept our role for what it is. Only the Lord knows exactly what His plan is for the specific client in front of us.

Because we live with our clients 24/7 for months, even years, we have learned that we cannot continually push them toward Jesus. It's like overwatering a plant. It can cause more harm in the long run. The Lord's way is always best, so when He says to be quiet, we trust Him in our silence. And when He says to speak, we trust Him to give us the words that will pierce her heart. We cannot possibly love our client better, more deeply, than the Lord Himself does.

So many times, I've seen new volunteers come in with a burning passion to save lost souls, only to become frustrated or disillusioned when no one's prayed a prayer of repentance by day 3.

I am 100% for lost souls being saved. It's the heart of the Father and it's my heart too. But it's not on our time schedule. It's on theirs. And only the Lord knows, with precision, exactly what that schedule looks like. And He has intentionally crafted each person's pathway to lead them to that point where they are primed to submit their will to His and surrender to His Lordship. Whether they will or not is their decision, but God faithfully creates the opportunities along their way.

My life verse is 2 Samuel 14:14 - Like water spilled on the ground, so we must die. BUT God does not take away life. Instead, He devises ways so that the banished will not remain estranged from Him.

I love Biblical BUTs, so that emphasis is obviously mine. The picture I get, as I read this verse, is of guardrails along a dangerous stretch of mountain highway. I lived in Colorado for several years and very quickly learned to appreciate the metal guardrails which prevented cars from driving off cliffs hundreds and thousands of feet in the air. Unlike a ditch that would cause more annoyance than harm, if I were to drive off a cliff it would be almost certainly fatal. And in some areas, the tree cover is so thick that it would have been nearly impossible for anyone to know it had happened.

God faithfully places guardrails along our life-journey to protect us, yes, and also to direct us. He guides our steps sometimes in the open road ahead and sometimes in the heavy barriers which prevent us from going in a wrong, sometimes fatal, direction. Trust Him to do that for the people you serve too.

3. **Accepting Their Version of Success**

The next challenge of a successful Restore process is understanding and accepting that one person's success is going to look far different than another's. For one person, success may be overcoming their addiction and enrolling in college. For someone else, it may be moving in with Grandma, allowing Grandma to help care for her children while Mom works to provide for the family.

Family looks different for everyone. So does success.

You certainly want to maintain basic ministry standards. I'm not saying that everyone should get a free pass to behave any way they choose and yet you still get to consider them a "success." But the flip side is also true—their path to lasting stability shouldn't be required to look a certain way or else their success is somehow suspect or inadequate.

Sometimes success will look like a homeless veteran connecting with his estranged son and moving in with his family. And sometimes, the estranged son refuses to acknowledge him. Sometimes, success is moving the vet into a small apartment, designed for men just like him, while other times, it is providing him a warm, dry tent so he can continue living independently.

Sometimes success looks like we think it should and other times, it looks very different than if we were the ones writing their happy ending.

Only in movies does the story end at a fixed, arbitrary point. In reality, their stories continue on for years, even decades. The Lord knows the plans He has for them, plans to prosper them and not to harm them. Plans which give them hope and a future. Because the Lord knows what it will take to bring them each to a place where they will call upon Him and come and pray to Him. He longs for the day when they arrive at His feet and He can listen to them, drawing them deeper toward Himself. (Jeremiah 29:11-13)

God is far more interested in their eternal salvation than we are. And we definitely are! Only God knows what actions we might take, in our zeal, that would be harmful to His plans.

One of the most painful examples of this principle is in the area of parents getting custody restored of their children, following addiction.

This is nearly always the desire of everyone in the situation, however, sometimes it happens too quickly and can cause major issues for everyone because of that. Or coming out of jail and now the family believes they are "fixed," and should be ready to be the adult they're supposed to be.

Let me tell you a fairly recent story, which should help you put all of this into perspective.

Rescue Rebuild Restore

A local ministry friend had seen where we were hiring some new staff and she had a candidate she wanted to send our way, once she was released from jail in a few days.

My ministry friend, "Beth," praised "Sarah" and how she had grown and matured while in jail. Sarah was active in Bible studies and proclaimed a strong relationship with the Lord. Beth felt she would be a perfect fit for the case manager role we were hiring for. When Sarah came in to interview, we knew immediately that she was not ready for employment—she still needed a great deal of support and healing.

So we invited her into our nonresidential program, which would have included employment, either in our job-training program or outside the ministry, once Sarah was ready for that phase.

Sarah thought the plan was great. She connected well with staff and other clients—some of whom she had known as a child (we're a small town). But Beth? Oh she was super pissed at me. She called almost immediately after Sarah left our offices. Beth said she couldn't believe I had misunderstood so badly. Sarah didn't need another program, she needed a job.

I kindly and politely (seriously, I was nice!) explained to Beth that Sarah was not ready for that level of responsibility. She still had a long way to go in her healing recovery journey. She needed support and equipping, not weighty responsibility.

But Beth knew best and decided to employ Sarah at her own ministry.

A couple years later, Sarah is now in prison for 10 years or longer and Beth is heartbroken.

The problem was that Beth couldn't see the value in our trauma-informed support. She so badly wanted Sarah to be "fixed" that she bypassed true healing, avoided hard conversations and focused instead on Christian busy-work as opposed to the deep work of recovery.

We see this frequently in parents who have custody of their grandchildren, as well. Mom gets out of jail or rehab and, rather than giving her time to acclimate to a sober lifestyle, the kids are back with Mom immediately.

What's challenging is that this is the exact outcome that is ultimately in everyone's best interest: Mom stable and raising her own kids, independent from grandparents. But not too fast.

People are often so quick to restore custody, seeking not to harm the kids, that they end up causing more harm by failing to wait until Mom is ready for that level of responsibility. And then, when she invariably fails, Mom and kids are traumatized all over again. Maintenance Mode is a powerful piece that's too easily skipped, sometimes with tragic results.

Preparing for Next Steps

The Restore phase is a permanent, ongoing process that never ends. Much like discipleship, there is always a lesson to learn, a new revelation to uncover. Growth Mode never ends. Encourage clients, graduates, and friends to embrace lifelong growth, as Proverbs 1:5 teaches, "Let the wise listen and add to their learning."

Learning something new everyday should be our default goal.

As we transition to the final section of this book, we'll explore implementing the Rescue, Rebuild, Restore Framework in your ministry. For now, let us pray for the humility to trust the Holy Spirit, accept free will, and celebrate diverse successes, anchored in God's love for lasting transformation.

Self-Assessment: Evaluating Your Restore Approach

Use this assessment to reflect on your approach to restoring. Rate each statement on a scale of 1-5 (1 = Strongly Disagree, 5 = Strongly Agree). Total your score to gauge your readiness and identify areas for growth.

- I trust the Holy Spirit to guide each receiver's path to restoration, even when their choices differ from my expectations.
- I accept that receivers have free will to make decisions—good or bad—without trying to control their outcomes.
- I celebrate incremental progress in receivers (e.g., shorter abusive cycles, small faith steps) as success, not failure.
- I recognize that each receiver's version of success may look different, avoiding rigid standards or ideals.
- I avoid pushing receivers toward salvation or change on my timeline, trusting God's perfect plan for their journey.
- I understand how poverty, trauma, addiction, or mental health shape receivers' decisions, responding with patience and grace.
- I maintain basic ministry standards but allow flexibility, ensuring receivers feel empowered, not judged.
- I pray for wisdom to discern my role—planting, watering, or celebrating growth—leaving increase to God.
- I remain committed to restoring, even when receivers relapse or leave, believing in their potential for God's best.

Scoring:
- 9-18: You may need to deepen your restore approach, seeking God's guidance to serve with trust and patience.
- 19-36: You're making progress, but there's room to refine your methods, focusing on autonomy and grace.

Rescue Rebuild Restore

- 37-45: Your restore approach is strong and faith-filled, but continue seeking His wisdom to sustain your ministry.

Chapter 10: Uniquely Serving

So how do we begin applying the Rescue, Rebuild, Restore Framework into ministries across the US?

As you can probably guess, this whole system is fraught with challenges and idiosyncrasies, which shift from one client to the next. This is not a design flaw but rather a *feature*. The reality is that everyone you serve is unique, with their own strengths and weaknesses, opportunities and areas where they could quickly fail.

There is no one-size-fits-all approach when it comes to working with other people. You must be willing to hold everything loosely, to allow for individualization of *almost* everything.

You will certainly have a few hard and fast, unbreakable rules, but those should be the few major deal-breakers, rather than lists of dozens of rules which can be easily broken and sporadically applied. You want your (few) rules to be hard and fast and the consequences to be clearly understood.

The biggest factor of whether someone is going to be successful with you is how much you can or will individualize your response to them. Programs which only provide a singular, fixed response, a cookie-cutter approach, are infinitely less successful in real outcomes.

Cookie-cutter programs are designed to benefit the organization, not the individual. A program can say they fed 400 families in a month with a box of food, but they cannot say they helped any of those families move beyond the financial situation which necessitated their request for a food box.

A cookie cutter program may say that they housed a young mom through her pregnancy until six weeks postpartum, but they cannot demonstrate that the mother and child are now living fully independent, not at risk of homelessness. This type of program is much easier to manage. Most state and federal programs are cookie cutter. The overarching assumption is that this promotes "fairness," for example, that a family of two should get $X in food stamps and a family of three should receive $X more.

However, if we do not factor in mom's ability to work, her health, her addiction history, and her mental health, as well as the father's involvement and the children's age, health, and allergies, then some women receive exactly the help they need, others receive more than necessary, and some receive far less than they need to survive.

It's not a *fair* system; it's merely easier to manage.

Honoring God's Unique Design in Every Soul

As followers of Christ, we are called to love the least of these with wisdom, compassion, and discernment—meeting each person where they are, not where we assume they should be.

Embrace the rugged, God-given uniqueness of every individual we serve, trusting that the Lord has crafted each soul with purpose, even in their brokenness. Individualizing programs and assistance for each client challenges your team to understand and address the deep-rooted issues of poverty, trauma, addiction, and mental health that shape their lives, tailoring care to their specific needs and stories.

The Heart of Individualization

The Bible reminds us in Psalm 139:14 that we are "fearfully and wonderfully made." No two people are alike—not in their struggles, their gifts, or their journey toward restoration. Yet, in our zeal to serve, it's tempting to apply a one-size-fits-all approach, offering programs or solutions that feel efficient but fail to address the deep, personal needs of each person. Tailored, individualized care calls us to reject this temptation, leaning into the Holy Spirit's guidance to see and serve each individual as Christ does—uniquely, deeply, and with unwavering love.

This approach becomes even more vital when we consider the complexities outlined in Chapter 6. Poverty, for instance, extends beyond material lack to include a poverty mindset—a worldview that sees only scarcity, not resources or opportunities. Some individuals we serve may live in chronic poverty, surrounded by food deserts, medical deserts, employment deserts, or educational deserts, where entire communities lack access to the basics needed for thriving. Others, even the wealthy, may carry a poverty mindset that blinds them to God's provision.

Individualized care invites us to listen to their story, assess their unique circumstances, and design support that addresses both their material needs and their mindset, helping them see the opportunities God places before them. For one person, this might mean connecting them to local job training programs that match their skills; for another, it could involve mentoring to shift their perspective toward abundance, trusting in the Lord's provision as we walk alongside them.

Trauma, too, requires a personalized response. As we discussed, trauma is multi-faceted, distinct from the event itself, and deeply affects the brain and body. The sympathetic nervous system (our "hot system," or survival mode) kicks in during trauma, preparing the body for immediate action—accelerating heart rate, constricting blood vessels, and raising blood pressure, muscle tension, and physical sensations. This response, while life-saving in the moment, can become chronic, leaving individuals stuck in a state of hypervigilance or emotional overwhelm.

Conversely, the parasympathetic nervous system (our "cool system," or growth mode) is where God designed us to function normally—promoting digestion, fuel storage, and resistance to infection while releasing endorphins to restore peace and balance. Chronic trauma, however, can harm brain and body development, creating barriers to healing. Tailored care means recognizing these differences: one person might need trauma-informed counseling to calm their "hot system" and rebuild trust, while another may require quiet, consistent support to gently reengage their "cool system" and rediscover growth.

Addiction, often rooted in the chronic pain of trauma, presents another layer of individuality. Drug usage may have started as a way to numb the unbearable pain of past wounds, but it escalates into addiction, bringing physical, mental, emotional, and relational consequences. While the physical addiction can be addressed through medical detox or treatment, the emotional connection to addiction—tied to deep-seated trauma or unmet needs—is far more difficult to break. For one client, this might mean intensive one-on-one mentoring to uncover the root causes of their pain and rebuild healthy coping mechanisms rooted in faith. For another, it could involve community support groups where they find belonging and accountability, trusting in God's strength to break the chains of addiction. Individualization allows us to see beyond the addiction to the person, crafting a path forward that honors their unique journey and God's redemptive power.

Mental health, though a sensitive topic, is another area where individualized care is essential. Partnering with local, like-minded professionals can provide the expertise we need, but we don't require years of university training to walk alongside someone with compassion. However, we must approach this wisely, ensuring we have a complete picture of their medical history—accessing records with their consent—to understand whether we're equipped to serve them or need to refer them to specialized care. For one person, mental health support might mean regular prayer and encouragement to manage anxiety, while for another, it could involve coordinating with a counselor to address depression or PTSD. Individualized care calls us to prayerfully discern each person's needs, trusting the Holy Spirit to guide us in loving them wisely and well.

The Challenge of Perpetually Starting Fresh

Embracing a system of personalized care isn't easy. It requires time, patience, and a willingness to step out of our comfort zones. In a world that often values efficiency and uniformity, taking the time to truly know and serve each person can feel daunting. We might worry about resources, time constraints, or the risk of failure—especially when faced with the complexities of poverty, trauma, addiction, and mental health.

But Scripture calls us to trust in the Lord's provision, as Proverbs 3:5-6 reminds us: "Trust in the Lord with all your heart, and do not lean on your own understanding." When we lean into God's wisdom, He equips us to see beyond surface needs and address the heart of each person's story.

This path also challenges us to confront our own biases and assumptions. We may assume we know what's best for someone based on their circumstances, but God sees what we cannot. Individualization invites us to listen—really listen—to the stories, dreams, and struggles of those we serve, allowing the Holy Spirit to guide us in crafting solutions that honor their dignity and potential.

Practical Steps for Your Ministry

So how do we live out this kind of individualized care in our churches and ministries? Here are a few steps to guide us:

1. Pray for Discernment: Begin with prayer, asking God to reveal the unique needs, gifts, and challenges—whether poverty, trauma, addiction, or mental health—of each person you serve. The Spirit's wisdom will lead you to see beyond the obvious.

2. Build Relationships: Take time to know each individual—ask questions, listen without judgment, and build trust. Relationships are the foundation of effective, individualized care, especially when addressing complex issues like chronic poverty or trauma.

3. <u>Customize Support</u>: Design programs and services that flex to meet specific needs. This might mean adjusting timelines, offering one-on-one mentoring, or partnering with community resources that align with a person's goals—whether it's job training, addiction recovery, or mental health support.

4. <u>Celebrate Uniqueness</u>: Recognize and affirm the God-given strengths in each person, even in their struggles. Whether it's a talent for art, a heart for children, or a quiet resilience, these gifts are part of God's plan for their restoration, even amidst poverty or addiction.

5. <u>Trust in God's Timing:</u> Understand that transformation is a journey, not a checklist. Be patient, trusting that God is working in ways we may not immediately see, especially as individuals heal from trauma or rebuild after chronic poverty.

6. <u>Partner Wisely</u>: When facing mental health or addiction challenges, collaborate with local professionals who share our faith-based values, ensuring we have the full picture—through medical records and open communication—to serve effectively or refer appropriately.

The Reward of Individualization

Living out the daily challenges of individualized care isn't just a ministry strategy—it's an act of worship. When we honor the unique design of each person, we reflect the image of a Creator who delights in diversity and individuality. We also open the door for true transformation, helping the least of these not just survive, but thrive in the purpose God has for them—breaking free from poverty mindsets, healing from trauma, overcoming addiction, and finding peace in mental health struggles.

Rescue Rebuild Restore

As church members, we are called to be hands and feet of Jesus, walking alongside those in need with compassion and wisdom. This system of meeting people where they are and tailoring everything to their actual, felt needs, reminds us that loving wisely means loving personally—seeing each soul as a masterpiece in progress, crafted by a loving God who never gives up on His children. In this rugged, beautiful work, we trust the Lord to guide us, rebuild broken lives, and restore hope, one unique heart at a time.

Part 3: How Now Shall We Live?

Chapter 11: Are You Safe?

Imagine you're at the church's benevolence center, and a new person walks in seeking help. They look nervous and a bit wary. As a volunteer, how do you approach them? First, you need to make sure that the physical space is welcoming—comfortable seating, soft lighting, maybe some plants or artwork that's not intimidating. But more importantly, your interaction with them should be trauma-informed.

The term "trauma-informed care" recognizes the prevalence of trauma and aims to avoid re-traumatizing the person. That means being empathetic, listening actively, and not asking intrusive questions right away. So, you might start by introducing yourself, explaining what the center does, and asking how you can help them today. Keep your voice calm and gentle, and give them space to speak at their own pace.

Now, if this person is living in poverty, they might feel ashamed or embarrassed about their situation. It's important to treat them with respect, without any judgment or pity. You can acknowledge their bravery in seeking help and assure them that everyone here is here to support them. Maybe offer them a cup of coffee and a seat, helping them feel like more than just a case number.

And if they have an entitlement mindset, they might expect help without any strings attached. While it's important to be compassionate, it's also crucial to set clear boundaries and expectations. They need to understand that help comes with responsibilities, like attending classes or volunteering. It's about striking a balance between compassion and responsibility. We want to help, but we also want to empower people to help themselves.

But safety goes beyond these interactions. We need to think about confidentiality and privacy too. People sharing sensitive issues, like mental health or addiction, need to know their information is safe. That means using secure record-keeping systems and training staff on confidentiality laws, like HIPAA, if applicable. Imagine if someone shared their story, and it got leaked—trust would be shattered, and they'd never come back.

Accessibility is another big one. Is your program open to everyone, considering diverse needs, like language barriers, disabilities, or cultural differences? Maybe offer translations for non-English speakers, or ensure the space is wheelchair-accessible. It's about making sure no one feels left out or excluded.

Building trusting relationships is key, especially for those with trauma. Trust doesn't happen overnight. It takes consistent follow-ups, showing up when you say you will, and being reliable. Maybe send a text to check in, or invite them to a church event where they can feel part of the community. It's those little things that show you care and help them feel safe.

Now, let's talk about setting realistic expectations. What are your goals for the help you're providing? Is it to provide immediate relief, like a meal or shelter for the night? Or is it to help someone achieve long-term stability, like finding a job or getting counseling? It's crucial to be honest with yourself and with the person you're helping about what you can and cannot do.

For example, giving $20 to a homeless person won't solve their housing problem, but it can help them get through the day. That's a realistic expectation. In your benevolence program, if you're offering job training, you need to be clear about what kind of jobs it can lead to and what the time commitment is. Don't promise the moon if you can't deliver—it can lead to disappointment and erode trust.

So, to create a safe place, you need to:
- Understand and accommodate each person's unique needs, especially related to trauma, poverty, and entitlement.
- Ensure confidentiality and privacy, using secure systems and trained staff.
- Make the program accessible and inclusive, considering diverse needs.
- Build trusting relationships through consistent, reliable support.
- Set and communicate realistic goals and expectations clearly.

How do you assess if your program is safe? Ask yourself:
- Does our program have training for staff and volunteers on trauma-informed care?
- Do we have protocols for handling sensitive information confidentially?
- Is our physical space accessible and welcoming to people from diverse backgrounds?
- Do we have mechanisms in place to address entitlement mentalities, like clear rules and expectations?
- How do we assess each person's unique needs and tailor our help accordingly?

Take a moment to reflect on these questions. Creating a safe place is an ongoing process, not a one-and-done deal. It requires continuous effort, learning, and adapting. But it's worth it, because when people feel safe, they're more likely to open up, engage, and start their journey toward healing and growth.

In the next chapter, we'll dive deeper into setting realistic goals and developing plans with the people you're helping. But for now, let's make sure that our foundation is solid—that we're providing a safe, supportive environment for everyone who walks through our doors.

Chapter 12: What Is Our Actual Goal?

As followers of Christ, we are called to love the least of these with wisdom, compassion, and humility—serving not from our own assumptions, but from a deep understanding of God's unique purpose for each person. In the RRR framework, developing systems and goals for our clients that align with their realistic abilities, rather than our preconceived ideas, is essential to true restoration.

Let's pause, pray, and partner with those we serve, ensuring our efforts lead to sustainable transformation rather than fleeting efforts. It challenges us to face the reality of their likely program completion—whether they move into a home of their own, return to drugs and crime, regain custody of their children, successfully complete our program, or quit, as they may have with so many other treatment programs before ours.

Understanding Their Exit Before We Bring Them In

Jesus met people where they were, but He also saw where they could be—guided by the Father's perfect plan. Before we invite someone into our programs or ministries, we must prayerfully consider their "exit"—the realistic, God-ordained destination for their journey with us. This means understanding the unique challenges they face, as outlined in Chapter 6, and crafting a path forward that honors their abilities, not ours, while accepting the hard realities of what their completion might look like.

For someone living in chronic poverty—whether in a material sense or a poverty mindset—we must assess the barriers they face, such as food deserts, employment deserts, or educational deserts, and determine what realistic progress looks like for them. Will they move into a home of their own, or will systemic barriers and a poverty mindset lead them back to instability? For a person wrestling with trauma, we need to recognize how their sympathetic nervous system (survival mode) may dominate their daily life, limiting their capacity to engage in certain goals. Will they find stability and growth, or will unresolved trauma trigger a return to old patterns, including drugs or crime?

Addiction, often rooted in the chronic pain of trauma, requires us to see beyond surface behaviors to the emotional and relational wounds, understanding that their exit might involve gradual steps toward sobriety—or, painfully, a relapse into addiction and its consequences, like criminal behavior. For those with mental health challenges, we must partner with professionals, review their medical history, and set goals that respect their current capacity, but we must also face the possibility that they might quit our program, as they have others, due to the overwhelming nature of their struggles.

Understanding their exit before we bring them in means starting with listening and prayer, not planning. It means asking, "Lord, what is Your goal for this person?" rather than imposing our own vision. It also means accepting the reality of their likely outcomes—whether success, relapse, or departure—while trusting God to work through every step of their journey. This honest assessment honors their dignity and sets them up for the most meaningful support, even if the path is challenging or uncertain.

Developing Realistic Goals in Partnership with the Individual

God calls us to walk alongside the least of these, not dictate their path. Developing realistic goals in partnership with each individual ensures that our systems reflect their unique strengths, struggles, and potential, guided by the Holy Spirit's wisdom. As Proverbs 15:22 reminds us, "Plans fail for lack of counsel, but with many advisers they succeed." We are not the sole architects of their restoration—our clients are co-laborers in God's work.

This partnership must account for the complexities of poverty, trauma, addiction, and mental health, while also facing the reality of their potential exits. For someone with a poverty mindset, a realistic goal might begin with small, achievable steps to recognize and access resources—perhaps connecting them with a job training program tailored to their skills. The hope may be that they eventually move into a home of their own, but we must also prepare for the possibility that systemic barriers or setbacks might delay or derail that outcome. For someone in trauma recovery, a goal might focus on building trust and safety, helping them transition from survival mode (sympathetic nervous system) to growth mode (parasympathetic nervous system), one day at a time, while acknowledging that unresolved trauma could lead them back to drugs, crime, or instability.

For those battling addiction, goals should address both physical dependency and the deeper emotional connections, setting milestones like attending support groups or rebuilding relationships, but we must also prepare for the risk of relapse or a return to criminal behavior, given the emotional complexity of addiction. And for individuals with mental health needs, goals should be developed in consultation with professionals, ensuring they align with medical insights and the person's current capacity, while recognizing that they might quit our program, as they have others, due to the overwhelming nature of their challenges or a lack of readiness for change.

This partnership requires humility, patience, and courage. We must listen to their dreams, fears, and limitations, then co-create goals that stretch them toward growth without overwhelming them—while also being honest about the potential outcomes, whether success or struggle. Realistic goals are not about lowering expectations but about aligning our vision with God's timing and their potential, trusting Him to do the heavy lifting, even in the face of setbacks.

Varying Levels of Responsibility, Rewarding Them for Investing in Themselves

God designed us for stewardship—caring for the gifts He's given us, including our time, talents, and opportunities. In our ministries, we can foster transformation by offering varying levels of responsibility and rewarding individuals for investing in themselves, reinforcing their dignity and agency. This approach not only builds confidence but also mirrors the biblical principle of sowing and reaping, as Galatians 6:7 teaches: "A man reaps what he sows."

Rescue Rebuild Restore

For someone in chronic poverty, this might mean starting with small responsibilities, like volunteering at a church event, and gradually increasing their role as they gain skills and confidence—rewarding their effort with encouragement, resources, or opportunities, while preparing for the possibility that they might not achieve housing stability or might face setbacks. For someone recovering from trauma, responsibilities could include participating in a support group, with rewards like recognition or mentorship, helping them feel valued and capable, but we must also be ready for the reality that they might return to drugs or crime if trauma overwhelms their progress.

For those in addiction recovery, responsibilities might involve accountability partnerships or community service, with rewards like certificates, community support, or leadership roles as they grow, while acknowledging the risk of relapse or departure from the program. And for individuals with mental health challenges, responsibilities should be tailored to their capacity, with rewards that affirm their progress and build hope, but we must face the likelihood that they might quit, as they have with other programs, due to the complexity of their needs.

By varying levels of responsibility and celebrating their investment, we help clients see themselves as active participants in their restoration, not passive recipients—even if their journey includes setbacks, relapse, or departure. This builds resilience, fosters ownership, and aligns with God's desire for them to thrive as stewards of His grace, no matter their exit.

The Reward of Aligning Our Goals with God's Purpose

Living out this approach—understanding their exit, developing realistic goals in partnership, and rewarding their investment—isn't just practical; it's an act of worship. When we align our goals with God's purpose for each person, we reflect His heart for restoration, rescuing them from despair, rebuilding their lives, and restoring their hope, even if their path includes relapse, quitting, or returning to old patterns. We trust the Lord to guide us, knowing that His plans are higher than ours, as Isaiah 55:8-9 assures us: "For my thoughts are not your thoughts, neither are your ways my ways, declares the Lord."

Accepting the reality of their likely program completion—whether they move into a home of their own, regain custody of their children, successfully complete our program, or face relapse, crime, or departure—requires faith and courage. It means loving them through every outcome, trusting that God is at work in their lives, even in failure or struggle. As church members, we are called to be hands and feet of Jesus, walking alongside the least of these with wisdom and love.

Our true aim is not to impose our ideals but to partner with God and each individual, crafting systems and goals that lead to lasting transformation—or provide grace and support in the face of setbacks—one unique, God-designed life at a time.

Chapter 13: Living the Framework

As followers of Christ, we are called to love the least of these with unwavering compassion, wisdom, and perseverance—transforming lives through the Rescue, Rebuild, Restore Framework. In this final chapter, we anchor in God's love, synthesize the journey we've explored, and equip you to implement this framework in your ministry with confidence and faith. Rooted in the challenges of poverty, trauma, addiction, and mental health, our mission is to rescue a generation, rebuild broken lives, and restore hope, trusting the Holy Spirit to guide every step.

The Heart of the Journey

Recall the prophetic dream from Chapter 7: an ocean of icy, choppy waters, a capsized ship, and my boat—anchored, stable, yet riding the waves—reaching down to lift fearful, struggling souls into safety. The boat expanded as the rescued became rescuers, pulling yet more from danger.

This vision exemplifies Foundation House's tagline: *Rescuing Mothers, Rebuilding Lives, Restoring Futures*, and reveals our call to rescue an entire generation of mothers, equipping them to save their children, celebrating when some children never need rescue at all.

This journey—Rescue, Rebuild, Restore—is not a linear checklist but a rhythmic dance of love, trust, and growth, tailored to each person's unique story. It begins with stabilizing in God's love, pulling others out of despair, building self-efficacy through trust, and empowering lasting transformation. Let's explore how these phases interlock, addressing poverty mindsets, trauma responses, addiction struggles, and mental health challenges, and how you can live this framework with courage.

Living Rescue, Rebuild, Restore Daily

The Rescue, Rebuild, Restore Framework is a holistic path to restoration, guided by unconditional love and individualized care:

- Rescue: Like lifting someone from icy waters, we stabilize, build trust, and gather data, pulling receivers out of poverty, trauma, or addiction with patience and grace. We avoid sustaining them with temporary aid, recognizing their readiness and brain and body differences (e.g., sympathetic nervous system activation), as Chapter 7 taught.
- Rebuild: Like adolescents learning to walk, we replace harmful patterns with new ones, fostering self-efficacy through mastery, encouragement, and role models, as Chapter 8 detailed. We navigate the Emotional Cycle of Change—Uninformed Optimism, Informed Pessimism, Valley of Despair, Informed Optimism, Success and Fulfillment—helping receivers push through fear or self-sabotage with trust.

- <u>Restore</u>: Like young adults taking ownership, we trust the Holy Spirit, accept free will, and celebrate diverse successes, as Chapter 9 described. We honor incremental progress, avoid control, and trust God's timing, even amidst relapse or resistance, knowing He devises ways for the banished to return (2 Samuel 14:14).

This cycle reflects God's heart for transformation, weaving together the insights from poverty mindsets, trauma, addiction, and mental health to create a trauma-informed, flexible approach.

Practical Steps for Implementation

Now, let's equip you to live this framework in your church or ministry. Here's a 6-step guide to begin:

1. <u>Assess Your Readiness</u>: Pray for discernment, evaluating your resources, staff training, and partnerships with professionals (e.g., for addiction, trauma, mental health). Use the self-assessments from previous chapters to identify gaps.

2. <u>Train in Trauma-Informed Care</u>: Equip your team with knowledge of poverty mindsets, trauma responses, addiction recovery, and mental health, using resources like those in Chapter 5's suggested cheat sheet or Chapter 7's brain science insights.

3. <u>Create Flexible, Individualized Policies:</u> Develop rules that prioritize safety but adapt to each receiver's needs, avoiding the pitfalls of Chapter 5's myths (e.g., more rules, more help, savior mentality).

4. <u>Build Trust and Gather Data</u>: Start with Rescue's stabilization, trust-building, and data-gathering, using tools

like Love Languages (Chapter 7) to tailor care, as in Chapter 3's giver-receiver dynamics.

5. Monitor Progress with Grace: Use the Emotional Cycle of Change (Chapter 8) to guide receivers through growth, celebrating small steps and accepting setbacks, as in Chapter 9's incremental progress.

6. Partner with God and Community: Trust the Holy Spirit to lead, as in Chapter 9, and collaborate with other churches, professionals, and sustainers (Chapter 7) for long-term impact, avoiding burnout (Chapter 4).

Consider this success story: A single mother, rescued from homelessness and addiction, rebuilt her self-efficacy through job training and support, then restored her life by regaining custody of her children, now mentoring others in your program. Her progress, though slow, reflects God's plan, inspiring your ministry to persevere.

Overcoming Obstacles

You may face doubts—time, resources, fear of failure, or past hurts (Chapter 3). But Philippians 4:13 assures us, "I can do all things through Christ who strengthens me." Here's how to overcome:

- Time and Money: Trust God's provision (Matthew 6:33), starting small with sustainers or community partners, focusing on one client at a time.
- Burnout: Count the cost (Chapter 4), leaning on prayer, community support, and realistic goals to sustain your energy.
- Fear of Failure: Accept free will and setbacks (Chapter 9), knowing God's plan transcends ours, as 2 Samuel 14:14 promises He devises ways for restoration.

- <u>Skepticism</u>: Reflect on the Emotional Cycle of Change—your Valley of Despair may lead to Informed Optimism, pushing through to fulfillment with faith.

Call to Long-Term Commitment

Living the RRR Framework is a lifelong act of worship, rescuing mothers to save their children, rebuilding communities, and restoring hope for generations. Matthew 25:40 declares, "Whatever you did for one of the least of these brothers and sisters of mine, you did for me," framing our ministry as service to Christ. Revelation 21:4 promises, "He will wipe every tear from their eyes… and there will be no more death or mourning or crying or pain," inspiring us to partner with God's eternal kingdom.

Anchor in His love, stabilize in His wisdom, and reach out with courage, knowing your boat will expand as the rescued become rescuers, transforming lives far beyond your ministry's walls. Trust Him to guide you through every wave, celebrating each unique success, even amidst poverty, trauma, addiction, or mental health struggles.

Closing Prayer and Charge

Lord, we come before You, dedicating our ministries to Your glory. Grant us the courage to rescue, rebuild, and restore with unconditional love, trusting Your timing and plan for each soul. Equip us with wisdom, patience, and grace to serve the least of these, seeing them as You do—fearfully and wonderfully made (Psalm 139:14). May our work ripple through families, communities, and generations, reflecting Your kingdom. We commit to this journey, anchored in Your love, in Jesus' name, Amen.

Go now, live the Rescue, Rebuild, Restore Framework as an act of worship, trusting God to transform lives, one unique heart at a time. You are His hands and feet—step boldly into His call.

Next Steps

What are your thoughts right now? As we wrap up this book, this time together, how are you feeling about everything I've shared with you?

What holes or gaps have you located within your current systems? What aha moments have cropped up? Have you already begun telling staff about what you've learned within these pages?

What will change when you close this book?

What do you *want* to change?

Do you feel like you have what you need to begin equipping staff, shifting systems, and seeing greater, more holistic, more sustainable client transformations?

So where do we go from here? You have two paths forward:

<u>Go it alone</u>: You absolutely have the capability to apply these strategies on your own. My greatest wish for you is that you understand how trauma, poverty mindset, addiction, and mental health affect your clients. It took me a decade of frustration as I dealt with client after client, consuming

countless books, videos, and a Master's degree, to learn everything I know today. To help you on your educational journey, I've included a list of books I recommend in the Resources section at the end of this book.

<u>Work with me</u>: If you prefer a customized approach, tailored specifically to your personal situation, I'm here to help. Together, we can integrate these strategies into your life, ensuring they work effectively for you, your home, and the mamas you serve.

You've read about several different ways in which BeCharityWise can help your team:

- Online (prerecorded) trainings
- Onsite trainings
- Coaching/consulting

They each have benefits and challenges, different levels of support and expense as you implement what you learn. Let me take a quick moment to explain the differences so you can determine exactly what fits your needs right now.

Online

We offer a wide range of recorded trainings in poverty mindset, trauma, addiction, case management, secondary trauma and self-care, plus we also do quarterly live trainings on topics that can be discussed in an hour or so. Pricing ranges from $99-$1999, depending on your needs and budget.

This option is best for those organizations who aren't ready for an in-person training, whether due to expense or time available, or you want to learn a specific topic together, as a team.

A major <u>pro</u> is the affordability, because it's all prerecorded. You own access to these recordings permanently, so future staff can benefit from them also. And, of course, a major <u>con</u> is that the information is all prerecorded... with no flexibility to discuss the nuances of your home. There's no coaching aspect to help you implement what you're learning.

On-site

We love visiting homes across the country, training and encouraging teams like yours!

This category is best for those organizations who are ready to take their training to a deeper level. They want to better understand the clients that are arriving and strengthen their processes so that the revolving door closes. They are ready for certification-level training and the whole team is prepared to be present for the <u>entire</u> event.

<u>Pros</u> are that you get to meet Lisa and me in person (sometimes other staff too) for three to five days. We individualize your training to ensure your team gains exactly what you need them to understand, training in all areas but focusing more heavily on the core aspects that your team most needs. We're able to answer questions and help you develop a plan to implement what you've learned after we're gone.

<u>Cons</u> are that it *is* more expensive, and those who aren't in the room together don't get the same level of knowledge and understanding. We don't mind being recorded but it isn't as effective when others watch the replays later. Especially when you're talking about three to five *days*' worth of video or audio.

Generally speaking, coaching is done with one or two individuals, while consulting is an organization-wide partnership, although there's plenty of overlap.

<u>Coaching</u> often looks like:

- Starting a new ministry or maternity home (Board development, fundraising, planning, staffing).
- Training new client services staff in their new roles with an established organization.
- Developing a more comprehensive intake process and training all staff in its use.

Consulting often looks like:

- An established pro-life organization adding housing to their services.
- Helping existing ministries reevaluate their services based on community needs: adding, removing, or re-designing programs such as job-training, nonresidential, childcare, addiction recovery, or adding multiple locations.

Our expertise accelerates your growth and expansion process while training and equipping you to serve mothers with far greater need levels, at the same time.

I would love to talk with you about how we can best help you accomplish your goals and serve your clients more effectively. For a personalized plan, email me at suzanne@becharitywise.com.

I'm here to support you on your journey toward a holistic trauma-informed ministry. You choose. Let's talk about it.

I'm happy to chat with you about what a Rescue, Rebuild, Restore™ training could look like for your ministry team.

Schedule a call with me when you're ready.

About the Author

Suzanne D Burns

MS, CFTP, CTII

Founder and Executive Director, Suzanne leads a thriving maternity home, with multiple sites and a social enterprise job-training program. Since opening in 2014, has housed over 150 mothers and served nearly 900 through non-residential services.

Internationally recognized speaker and trainer, podcast host, author of six books on ministry startup and trauma-informed care, Suzanne and her team have trained hundreds of organizations to implement practical tools to serve "the least of these" more effectively.

Foundation House Ministries is a faith-based maternity home and training program for pregnant and parenting women in critical situations. They have opened a job-training program, consisting of a thrift shop and they also make lotions, soaps, and candles, through their manufacturing side.

Suzanne has a Master of Science in Marriage and Family Studies from Lee University in Cleveland, Tennessee, and is a

Certified Family Trauma Professional. She is a member of the International Association of Trauma Professionals and the American Academy of Experts in Traumatic Stress. She serves as a member of the Leadership Council of the National Maternity Housing Coalition and the Executive Council for the Tennessee Commission on Children and Youth.

Suzanne regularly speaks regionally and nationally on the multi-faceted topics of chronic trauma, chronic poverty, addiction and the women that Foundation House serves. She provides executive coaching and training on these and other topics at becharitywise.com

Suzanne and her husband, Tim, reside in Cleveland, TN, with their younger son, Ethan, and his wife, Stevi. Their older son, Kaden, Suzanne's own crisis pregnancy, is married to Alexandria and they have two children. Their daughter, Carly, is married to Alex and they have two boys.

Rescue Rebuild Restore
Suzanne's Links:
https://facebook.com/becharitywise
http://www.becharitywise.com
Podcast:
https://podcasters.spotify.com/pod/show/trauminformedchurch
https://youtube.com/traumainformedchurch
Ministry Links:
Http://facebook.com/foundationhouseministries
http://instagram.com/foundationhm

Bibliography / Recommended Reading

A Framework for Understanding Poverty, Ruby Payne
Bait of Satan, John Bevere
Lost Connections, Johann Hari
Switch on Your Brain, Dr. Caroline Leaf
Teaching with Poverty in Mind, Eric Jensen
The Body Keeps the Score, Bessel van der Kolk
The Five Love Languages, Gary Chapman
Toxic Charity, Robert Lupton
When Helping Hurts, Steve Corbett and Brian Fikkert

(These are each Amazon Affiliate links. No additional cost to you, but every time you purchase from one of these links, I earn a small commission. Another way we serve more moms in crisis is through education.)

Made in the USA
Columbia, SC
13 March 2025